NO PROBLEM

EDWARD PRYNN

NO PROBLEM

The Story of a Cornishman
Part II

Edited by Jo Park

TABB HOUSE
1982

First Published in 1982
by Tabb House, 11 Church Street, Padstow, Cornwall, PL28 8BG.

Copyright © Edward Prynn and © Jo Park
ISBN   0   907018   16   5

Printed in Great Britain by Quintrell & Co. Ltd., Wadebridge, Cornwall.
Bound by R. Booth (Bookbinders) Ltd, Carnstead, Mabe, Cornwall.

Foreword

READERS OF *A Boy in Hob-Nailed Boots* will know how Edward Prynn, never having learnt to read or write, determined to become the author, if not writer, of books, and how I became involved with helping him to get his words into print. All his tapes and the full transcript have been lodged at the Institute of Cornish Studies at Pool.

Edward was born in 1936. *No Problem* begins in his eighteenth year; he had left school, had several jobs, and been delighted to find he was not fit for National Service, which meant he could stay in Cornwall, 'home in the place where I belonged', with his girl friend, Marie, an Italian *au pair*.

Edward and I have tried to contact all those mentioned in his life story. We thank those who have given their permission to publish Edward's memories of them, and English China Clays PLC, Mr Paul Spencer, Mr Jack Ingrey, Mr Desmond Logan, Mr Trevor England, Mr Donald Dark, and Edward's family for permission to reproduce photographs belonging to them.

Jo Park
31st March, 1982

Contents

List of Illustrations

CHAPTER 1

A Shot-Gun Job

THERE WAS ONE THING for sure, my love for Marie was very strong. I used to see her three times a week and when I wasn't with her I always used to be thinking about her, all the time. I suppose that's what love is about.

By this time we could talk; we could converse with one another. I wouldn't say she could talk good English, but she could get by, because she had been to a convent school. She told me all about how strict people and her parents were, in Italy. how she wouldn't be allowed to go out at home unless she had a chaperone.

She also told me that a girl is expected to be a virgin when she's married. And if she isn't her husband will chuck her out. I thought to myself: 'Well, they're pretty strong rules, when several people around here would have to get married.'

The courting was going well, but I know I arrived at The Old Mansion about eight o'clock one evening. The other girl had gone out. Marie was in, on her own, crying. I asked her what was the matter. She broke the news to me. She said: "I'm going to have a baby."

I couldn't believe it. I said: "Are you sure?" "Yes," she replied. God Almighty! And after what she'd told me what they were like out in Italy! I didn't know what my mother and father would say about the idea. I'd never bargained on this.

Well, we didn't plan on doing much, not just for a month or so; we'd keep it a secret. We wanted to confirm the situation, and so we waited a little while. I remember, one night, just before I was going courting, my father called me in the sitting room for what I suppose you'd call a little, fatherly talk. He said: "Edward, I don't want to know your business with this girl. If you're having an affair with her," he said, "be careful." He said: "If you ain't, well it doesn't matter, but you know enough about sex to make it very dangerous for yourself." The thing was, his advice came a bit too late. He was right in what he said. I'd got myself into more trouble than I'd ever anticipated. I wouldn't ever want to go through that experience ever again. I'd got involved in a shot-gun job.

I told Marie that we'd fix the date for getting married. It was about April time now, when I left Mr Parkyn to get a job in the quarry, 'cos you couldn't get a man's wage until you were twenty-one on a farm. At the quarry I was to break stones with a sledge hammer and I was working a lot of overtime. I told Mother I was getting married (Marie had been to this house on a few occasions and Mother liked her very much). I said: "On the 20th of July." Mother replied: "When? Next Year?" "No," I said: "this year." "Gaw! Quickly," she says: "There isn't anything wrong, is there?" "No," I said: "honest there isn't." Because mothers or parents don't like — they still don't, doesn't matter where you live — anything like that to happen in the family. Some people don't take much notice of it, but I think deep down they nearly all do.

Marie's parents wanted to know if there was anything wrong and she told them there wasn't.

All right, we all know you've got to get married where the bride wants to, you give her the choice and you'll be married in that place. Marie was a Catholic. Well, that was fair enough: I didn't care which her church was, if it was a Jewish church or any church. A marriage to me is a ring on your finger; churches or different religions don't bother me. Marie said: "It isn't so easy as that." She told me: "The Catholic priest wants to come and see you and give you seven lessons on the Catholic faith." Well, it was time I couldn't afford to give up, to come and see this priest. But Marie insisted, so I had to.

I know, on the first occasion, he told me that what children we had would have to be brought up in the Catholic faith. We couldn't be married in any other church because the Catholics would never recognise the marriage. And I forget the others. They were a lot of stringent rules. I remember saying to the priest: "Father, I'll sign this bit of paper and we'll forget all the lessons. Who's going to be the wiser?" He wouldn't hear of it. He made me have these seven hours, an hour a night it was.

Well, there you are, the road was clear. I was in, and going to be married on the 20th of July.

My brother was fully occupied because he was going to be the best man. My full names are Edward Christopher Hamley Prynn. I could spell Edward and Prynn all right, but I didn't know how to spell the others, and I knew this had to go on the Marriage Lines. I didn't want Marie to know about this, I tried to shield it from her. I felt ashamed. My brother taught me, wrote it out for me, my names. He printed it out big, and I learned it. In a few nights, I'd learnt it. He often used to say to me: "Can you spell it?" And yes, I could: no problem! But you start to lose confidence in yourself and you think: 'Will I dry up when the others are there, watching everything?'

Mother was busy organising the wedding. She never had a daughter and this was the best thing that could ever happen for Mother. She was delighted with the idea. She wanted four bride's maids. We often used to have little rows about it. I used to say: "Mother, I just want the most quietest wedding there ever is, with no guests or nobody. Only two bride's maids." The time was getting near. They'd bought the bride's maids' dresses. Marie was almost getting the wedding dress. I was busy, working, getting the money in.

Round in the village everybody was nattering about this shot-gun wedding. If I'd fooled Mother and Father, I hadn't fooled the village. The next thing we had to do (we left it pretty late), was buy an engagement ring. I was pretty excited about that. I bought one with three stones. I chose it. And then, a few weeks later we went back to get the wedding ring. Marie bought me one was well. I really felt so excited when we bought the wedding rings; that was the highlight of the whole job. I really felt the marriage was secure. It didn't matter about whoever the vicar or minister was. I thought we'd completed the deal in the shop now. We were like a sailing ship really on its right course. There was nothing to stop us.

I know the presents began to roll in from everybody in the village. I think they just wanted to help us along a bit, to give us a start. They gave Marie and me everything. Even Boss Hammett* sent a present down, on behalf of him and his staff. It was all go.

* An employer of Edward's — See Part I

I think poor Marie thought to herself: 'Well, nobody hasn't sent anything from Italy.' Which I don't think they did. She never had any of her people there, but Mother was so thrilled about the whole lot. I can tell you, my mother was over the top with it.

I know, the night of the wedding, Marie came, brought all her cases, because after we were married we were going to live here at Trevithick Estate, at No.8 where I live now. She came by taxi, and she had one case all full of sheets, pillow slips, blankets and all the little knick-knacks that she could get. She only used to earn £1.0.0d. a week. I almost cried when she opened her case. I couldn't believe it, to think that she had no mother or anybody to help her and yet she had all this bedding and other things. I looked at her: Marie shone like a giant light in a forest. She'd lead you through anything, that's the sort of woman she was.

I know there was one old Scots lady that lived around here who said it was pretty unlucky to see the bride once you'd said 'Goodnight' on the night before the wedding. It was no good for me to see Marie in the morning. The next time I had to see her was at the altar. So Marie had to go down and sleep at Mrs Martin's house, in Trevithick.

I didn't sleep all that night. I was thinking about everything. I never even told my brother about this baby. But morning came around. Brother and I had got the beer from the pub. It cost father, at that time, I should think about £50 or £60. They paid for the wedding, my parents.

But the big day was on. Father looked at me in the back kitchen and he says: "Boy, you're looking miserable." "No," I says: "I'm all right." He says: "You enjoy it, this is the happiest day of your life." Our next-door neighbour drove us to Padstow. He was a policeman at St Merryn Royal Naval Air Station. He was a Plymouth man and, instead of going straight to Padstow, he made a little detour and went to Harlyn Bay first. I looked out over, 'cos that's the place where Marie and I did all our courting. I just thought of the happy times we had there on the beach. But on we go to Padstow.

Well, you all know what weddings are about. Brother and I were there well before time. We waited. I didn't think Marie was coming. I heard somebody say: "She's now come." The church was full. Nearly everybody came from my village. It's fantastic as I look back over it and think of that. I know, I looked behind and saw Marie come, walking up the aisle. Captain Miller gave her away, the Boss that owned The Mansion. I caught hold of her hand and held her tight. To catch somebody hold by the hand and hold them tight makes you feel that you're going to save them. It's going to be all right and that's what I was going to do. I wasn't going to let this girl down.

The priest started to go through the service. Marie cried all the time. I don't think she got the words right at all, not the bits 'I do' and this and that. To be quite honest, I can't remember much about it. It was all like a haze to me, the whole lot. The only thing I remember is putting the wedding ring onto Marie's finger. And that was good enough for me. I had done it then. It didn't matter whose church we were in. That was it. She was mine and I was going to do my best for her.

We went off to the little vestry to sign the Marriage Lines thing. It was a huge, great, long piece of paper. My brother stood behind me just in case I was stuck. But I got through my names pretty well. The others were talking away fair, and it was all over.

There's always one person that comes to a wedding that you remember, and at mine it was Mrs Dingle from our village, and she lives there now. She was waiting by the door and as I came out she just gave me a kiss and wished me and Marie luck. That was good.

Captain had brought the Rolls Royce. In Marie jumps and me, and away we go. I came home from Padstow. I went in an old Hillman and I came home in a lovely, great Rolls Royce! I don't know how Mother had fitted everybody into No.8 and catered for everybody, but I suppose as weddings go it was perfect. I had a few telegrams. I was worried about that; thought I might have to read them. But, as I know now, the best man reads the telegrams. Marie and I, we were both nervous and knew my mother had to find out eventually, but we decided we'd never tell Marie's parents about it. She would never be allowed back there if they ever knew about this.

Marie and I changed. I had this new suit to be married in, but I'd bought one off a chap out in the quarry for a pound, a brown suit, and we went off. By the time I had settled everybody up, all

I had on me was £7.10s.0d. And then we went off to Padstow Station. Once more, we rode in the Hillman. Several people came to see us off. They really did. That was one of the best things of all the wedding, what the people of my little village gave me.

We were in the train. It was a steam train. Marie wore a brown and yellow little square dress. I can't describe dresses very well. We set off. We were going to my Auntie up in Paignton, that's near Torquay. We left about five o'clock and we got there at half-past-nine in the evening. It was the first time my auntie was ever to see Marie. My auntie was a Port Isaac girl who married someone from Paignton and went there to live. My uncle met us at the station and we went up to the house; Auntie made us tea and started to talk to Marie. My Uncle Joe caught me on the side, he said: "Is there anything wrong?" "No," I said: "Not at all." "Well," he said: "Bit quick, isn't it?" I said: "Yes, it's a bit quick, but there's nothing wrong." "All right," he says.

Well, honeymoons; I don't want to take you through that lot; they're the same for everybody. I know I only had about three day's holiday. I started work right on the Saturday. I was lucky, there was plenty of overtime going.

I know, we weren't exactly fixed up for a bed properly, and that Sunday I went back to Mr Parkyn, where I had worked, to get some bed irons. I had a good bed, but the irons weren't good enough. And he turned out this old bundle of bed irons. It was a hard job to get a pair, but in the end we found a pair. And I got fixed up properly with a bed.

CHAPTER 2

The Rock Fall

MARIE AND MOTHER were getting on like a dream. She accepted her as her own daughter. Father accepted her as well, like a daughter. She was never a stranger. I was a bit afraid the village people wouldn't accept her, as she was an *I-talian*, but they did so because she'd married a Cornish chap. So all was well that way.

I know three weeks had passed by and one morning Marie was not too good. She and Mother had got up to get me off; and Mother was working at that time, and my brother was home as well. Marie was sick and went back to bed. Mother said: "Is there anything wrong?" I never answered. I picked up my dinner bag and my coat, and just as I was leaving the door, I said: "Yes, Mother, there is something wrong." I couldn't carry on any longer with it now. Mother's face dropped. She said: "Is Marie going to have a baby?" I said: "Yes." "Oh! All right," she says: "When?" Mother thought it happened on the honeymoon, I think. I said: "The baby will be here for a Christmas present." Poor old mother cried. I went out the door. But I do know Mother went to Marie's room and told her it didn't matter: "Don't worry about it, it might be a girl." We haven't had a girl in the Prynn family for a long, long time. She only wished Marie had told her before and saved all the worry.

So now that big burden was off my shoulders. It was all free, home here. Marie wasn't so happy about it, but as her family lived all those miles away in Italy, it didn't really matter. Everybody started to make baby clothes for us and gave us little things to get ready for the baby, because we didn't keep it a secret any longer. Even the bride's maids were so delighted. It was unbelievable.

Back at the quarry, things were really going strong. I can't set your hearts a-glow with quarry work, but I can tell you what takes place in the tea hut at crib times and dinner times. There were about twelve to fourteen men there, and there was one old chap that had been married for a long, long time. He was called Old Fred Thomas. We called him by a nick-name, Old Pal, because it was an expression he used to use. He was about sixty-three, or four; he'd finished lorry driving and he was just making out his time in the quarry. He used to say to me: "Edward, have you had any rows yet?" "No, Fred, or ain't likely to. We're in love, we'll never row." "Well," he said: "it'll happen eventually. You're young," he said: "and you wouldn't know how to handle things. I'm going to give you a little advice, what to do when it happens." He said: "A woman, Ed, have got queer ways of breaking a man. You know what a little bit of dynamite can do to one of those big stones? Smash it to smithereens." He said: "That's what a woman can do to a man, if she start working on him." And he said: "They've got cruel ways of doing it. You don't know it's happening. But," he said: "when this row takes place, the first thing that she'll want to do is pack her bags and go home." I listened to Fred. He said: "And when she says she's going home, I don't want you to lose your temper one little bit. You're to help to pack those cases, write the labels and make all the arrangements, so it's easy." I said: "Fred, this will never work, it don't seem right to me." "Well," he said: "If you get a young cow and you can't get her in the yard, the more you try and get her in the worse it make her. If you leave the gate open, she'll come back on her own." I laughed to myself. I said: "All right, Fred, I'll bear that in mind."

Anyhow, we were pretty happy. Things were going along pretty good. It was dangerous work for me in the quarry. There were safety goggles provided, but I never wore them. Stones used to go around my forehead. But there, I took the chance and that was it. I never thought about it. I got promotion to be shovel driver.

In our dinner times — I ain't afraid to tell you now — we used to go down and take dynamite and blast and catch ourselves a few fish. We were never short of fish. It was good: you could look seawards way down to Constantine, Treyarnon and Bedruthan Steps; you could see the Quies and the Gulland Rock. You'd see the boats out at sea, picking up their crab pots.

You'd see them there on rough weather and on calm weather. There were a few holiday-makers around as well. You just imagine, if you brought your office or factory right touching the seaside, and you had it for all the year! We used to go bathing in the dinner time, in summer. Winter time, we used to go wrecking.

I know we had one chap come along, John; he was a farm labourer and he soon got promotion to be a driller. Also his brother worked at the quarry. We were a happy little gang. John used to be my mate. Dinner times we often used to go fishing. We had our crab pots down at Trevose Head and we used to carry them down and sling them out over into the water and when it came tea-break we used to climb down the cliff, down at Mackerel Cove, and have a look and see what was doing. He was a great person.

The face where we were working was like this: about sixty yards wide, but it ran up nearly from the bottom of the quarry face almost to the top and the last fifteen foot, at the top, the hard blue elvan stone stopped and there lay a wall of brown stone, sitting on top of this big slide. My mate had been up a couple of days before and started to work this new face. He started to bore his holes there, at the bottom of the brown, and we were going to blast and work this big slide down, to get all the best stone.

I remember, it was a beautiful morning. And when we had blasted, there was a lot of loose rock still left up there, and my mate went back with a crow-bar, just to get it all off and make it safe, and I kept looking up. It was as if something strange had happened to the face, but I didn't know what. I could see little trickles of stone and dust trickling down. You know, we've all seen Westerns: a little puff of smoke is a warning of trouble. Well, that's what I was seeing, but I didn't know what the messages meant. There, I carried on as usual. I was loading stones into the mechanical shovel with my mate's brother. I looked up and I saw the whole damn, giant face bursting. I can see John there now. I said to his brother: "Look, look at John." And he looked up too. By now it was like seeing a blind man standing on a railway line and trying to warn him that the train was coming; but it was no good, he didn't know what to do, where to run exactly. He ran down this slope. He

picked a point where there was about a twenty foot drop. He
was ahead of the rock fall then and he just had to jump for his
life. I can see him now. He was like a parachutist. That was the
last we saw of him. The loose boulders and rocks and dust just
piled John right to the ground. That was it.

All that noise and shouting for about a second. It was all over.
The dust rose in the quarry, 'cos it was summer time. There it
was, it was just as if you'd raked the garden: the big boulders
right out in the front and all the fine, loose stones lying on top,
on top of my mate. I think the Lord Himself had buried John
there.

Instantly we ran forward to the great rock pile. We started
digging with shovels. John's brother, he really cried. A man's
entitled to cry when he sees something like that. He kept
repeating: "Answer me, boy, answer me." In the end, one of the
others led him away and said: "That's it. He's had it." I was so
afraid with the shovel, I might just drive right in and kill him,
but after an hour's digging we didn't find him. I asked someone
else if he would drive the shovel. Soon they found John and
they put him in the ambulance and took him away.

When I went that lunchtime, there was my mate's dinner bag
with his flask and his tin that his wife had packed off in the
morning. John was going to pick her a bunch of flowers that
night; he had told me on the way out in the lorry that morning.
When I went down to the crab pots, on my own next time, there
was his crab pot still there. He was a long way away in Heaven
then.

I'm not laying blame on anybody, not bosses, workmen or
anybody at the quarry. Some years ago, maybe, workers worked
a bit dangerously, and so did bosses. By the Grace of God that's
all changed. We're all safety conscious, which is as it should be.
But I tell you to remind you that your employees are looked
after, or the ordinary workers themselves should always remember
to be safe.

Like lots of things that happen, you talk about them a long
time after. There's a chap in this village called Les Martyn. Les
told me: "See boy," he said: "a rock face will talk just like we
humans. It doesn't talk with a voice, but it talk a different way."
He said: "You get little bits, just like a sixpence falling out the

side, little trickles of dust running down. Instead of seeing it smooth, you see it rough. That's sort of talking to you, saying: 'Well, look, I'm going to fall in eventually, get prepared!' That information came too late for me. I could most probably have saved my mate's life because I'd seen the talking. I'd seen the signals, the little bits of stone falling out the face. I saw this and didn't know what it meant.

But Christmas was coming on. I was a bit excited. And on 29th December Marie was taken ill, I suppose about ten or eleven o'clock at night. A sou'west wind was blowing from Land's End. It was a terrible night. This house almost shook. Our nurse, called Nurse Docherty, lived only a couple of doors away. She came. About a quarter-to-twelve, we were all downstairs, my brother, father and mother, waiting and we heard the baby cry! Mother said: "What is it? Is it all right?" Nurse said: "It's all right and it's a boy."

CHAPTER 3

Christopher John Prynn

YES, A SON. I had a son. I was nineteen years of age and he had turned up, right there. Nurse told me to go and telephone Doctor Alken who lived down at Constantine Bay. I was shaking like a leaf — a jelly-fish. I rode my bike down to Shop. There was no 'phone here then. I told him everything was all right, but Nurse needed him right away back at Trevithick. I got back as the Doctor was there. And after an hour we were allowed to see the baby. Oh! My mother was thrilled, and we really all were.

She and Marie had picked out the names beforehand, unknown to me. I didn't have any choosing in that at all. We called my new son Christopher John, that was after his uncle, and one of my names. Christopher John Prynn. That was one thing that I was against. I said: "Just make it one Christian name. That's all." I didn't want a load of names 'cos I was worried: I didn't want my son to be a dunce like me, or, if he should have to be, he wouldn't have so many names to write. But, all right, it had to be two.

I know it wasn't to be long before I was out on the road, with the pram. I'd given up, long gone now, going out with the other boys and meeting down on Shop Corner, with all our push-bikes, going off to Padstow Pictures with the gang and down to beach and all that. I remember, my first time out with the pram, the others were down on Shop Corner and one or two of them, just for fun, said: "'Ello, Ed: You've got a good pair of wheels, what are you carrying?" They knew what I was carrying all right, but I didn't care. I had my boy and I was happy.

But there was a bit of a slump in the building trade, and I had a week's notice to quit.

I was lucky. One of the lorry drivers got me in the back door. He knew a foreman with another firm, a well-known company, and I joined Costain's on a pipe track here in this village and

back out towards Trevose Head, to take the water for the
Coastguard Station. Pick and shovelling now. That's hard going.
But that didn't make any difference to me, if it wasn't reading
and writing. I could dig a hole in the ground faster than some
guys could write a sixty thousand *letter* book. It was no problem
to me. I enjoyed work.

I met there with an all Padstow gang. There was nobody
from St Merryn at all. I made friends with a chap called Tom
Bate; he is dead and gone now; he died of leukaemia. Tom was a
fisherman, he loved it, but he couldn't get a berth on a ship so he
had to come digging trenches with me. It sometimes happens in
life; the wrong chaps are doing the wrong jobs, but there's
nothing they can do about it. We used to talk of the sea.

I know, at one stage, I said to Marie: "I'm going to try and get
a boat and I'm going to sea with Tom." But she wouldn't have it.
She really loved me; she couldn't just bear for me to go. But I
would, almost . . . I loved the sea. You can love the sea as much
as you can love a woman. But Marie was good for me. We all
know in life marriage is like a partnership. It's something like a
motor boat: you need an engine for power and a rudder to steer it.
In our case, I was the engine and Marie was the rudder. She was
going to guide me in anything I did.

Marie had a tremendous gift of surprising me. She's the only
person who could ever do it. I know I was riding my bike miles
to get to work. I had a good old bike. One night I came home from
work: she'd got me a brand new one! It was the first brand new
bike I'd ever had in my life! I was really pleased about it.

The boy was growing away good. Marie was working. With
Marie and Mother, there was never a problem from the word
go. She must have been the only *I-talian* that could ever talk the
proper Cornish language. She learnt to bake pasties and cook
just like Mother. If Mother was bad Marie could carry on. You
couldn't tell the difference, who cooked the meals. It was
happiness for Mother, as she had never had it in her life.

I was working at Dinham's Bridge, near Wadebridge. I was
on one side of the road, down this hill, digging with pick and
shovel and another friend of mine from Padstow, was the other
side, and it was too far for us to talk to one another. The
foreman came to see us and he turned around and went up the

road, and I dropped my pick and shovel and I walked back to where this other chap was. Foreman came down, round the corner and caught me. He told me to come right up to the office and pick up my cards. I'd had the sack, and it was my own fault. I'd broken the rules and left my post. There were plenty of men knocking around at that time.

Marie and my father and mother played hell about it. But I was lucky, and got in the back door again with another construction firm, working down Falmouth this time, on a sewerage job. Once more I was earning good wages. We bought our first car. An old Wolseley. I had a chap in the village that taught me to drive. Or not exactly taught me to drive; I could drive anything, but this was going to be different. I never told him that I couldn't read nor write. I insisted: I went over the course at Bodmin every time. That's where the test was going to take place. I knew every bit of Bodmin. I got my father to read the Highway Code for me. He read it on three occasions, and at that time I could tell you everything in the Highway Code backwards.

But the day of the test came. I failed, because I never gave my hand signals right! Nothing wrong with the Highway Code.* I put in for a *cancellation* and I know it was a matter of a fortnight until I was back up there again. I passed with flying colours and the man asked me a lot of questions on the Highway Code. It was just like water running out of a tap, that's how easy it was. You couldn't stop it. I said: "Have I passed?" He said: "Yes, you have. Sign here," he says. I signed my name, just Edward Prynn. I was shaking like a leaf. Marie and everybody were pleased I'd passed my test. At least I could take them all out in the car now. By this time a lot of people were getting cars.

We hadn't had any big rows; just little, small ones; but soon after that a big one happened, over something trivial that I can hardly remember. I thought: 'God! It's just happened like Fred predicted.' I remembered everything he'd told me. She said: "I'm packing my bags and going." I said: "All right, dear. If you don't want to stop, I won't stand in your way." I said: "You're not taking the boy though." "No," she said: "I understand that."

*Edward could distinguish numbers and letters sufficiently for the 'Number Plate at a Distance' part of the test

I said: "I'll help you to pack." I got the two cases down from the loft and put them on the bed. I got the dresses out of the wardrobe and started to put them in nicely. I know at one stage she said: "Oh no, I'll do that." But I insisted that I would as well. I told her that I was going across the road, because the 'phone box was fitted on this estate by that time. I said: "I'm going to 'phone Bodmin Road and find out the times of the train." "All right," she says. I can tell you, I didn't like doing it. It wasn't the way I would actually work. I was working under instructions from Fred, because he was a bit of an expert on these matters. Fred told me: "They won't go. Just be nice and don't lose your temper." Well that's *zactly* how I worked it. I told her she could come home. I said: "The door's open for you, my love, anytime you want to. I don't want you to go, but if you want to, well, all right, I can't stand in your way."

We packed up everything. Mother and father were screeching, and it was a right old do, I can tell you, but I was cool as a cucumber. Loaded the cases into the car. Marie said "Good-bye" to her son and away we went. I tell you, I was almost ready to chicken out of the lot, but I thought 'Maybe she will, eventually. I won't give in.' We jumped in the car and started to drive towards Bodmin. I got to the corner that turned off for Harlyn Bay. I thought: 'To hell with it!' I said: "To hell with it, Marie, if you want to go home, you've got to make your own arrangements!" I swung the car to the left and headed back to Harlyn Bay. She started laughing to herself and we went down to Harlyn Bay, where we did our courting, and made things up. I did see Fred, and told him what had happened. Fred said: "You should have took her right to Bodmin Road. She would have given in in the end." But there: I told you I was soft. So now you really know it. I couldn't go through with that when the crunch came.

CHAPTER 4

St Merryn to Naples

I KNOW IT CAME UP for me to reach the age of twenty-one, or almost, and we planned to go to Italy. There weren't too many people then, only very rich people, that travelled abroad. Boss Nancarrow* had told me a lot about Italy. He'd read us a lot. I knew about Mount Vesuvius and Capri and the Coliseum, Venice and all that. I knew of the Great Masters, painters, sculptors that lived there and some of the great Popes. Italy was a special place for me, and now, at last, I was going.

I told everybody I was going and here, in the village, maybe they'd forget it for a week or two, and then they'd say: "Well, Ed, when are you off?" "In another month." "Oh, yes! All right then." What they want to know really is, when you're coming back, to hear the tales you'll bring home.

But the big time came, and as it would be my twenty-first birthday in Italy, we must have left a week or so before 25th September. We went off from Bodmin Road. One of my neighbours took me; Marie and I got on the train — we had decided not to take Christopher. We thought it was a bad idea as we didn't know what sort of reception we would get from the other end, and as Richard† and his girl friend had told me how hostile they were, I was a bit nervous about this lot and what reception we were going to have. We'd say he was too young to take because he was only one year old (but really he was two years old).

The guard blew the whistle at the last train out of Bodmin Road to go to London that day; we'd be there by the morning. Mother and a few friends saw us off. Marie slept for most of the journey. I didn't sleep at all, I was so excited thinking that we were going to Italy. What the head stockman at Trevibban

*Edward's village school teacher — see Part I

†Richard introduced Edward to Marie — see Part I; his girl was Marie's *au pair* friend (see p.1)

Farm* had told me about *I-talian* girls and Italy had come true.

We arrived in London about six o'clock in the morning. We had a little bit of breakfast at the station, then we caught a taxi to Victoria Station. We caught the train for a little port called Newhaven. There we boarded the boat, and it wasn't long before we cast off and started gently to move out into the English Channel. Once out of the harbour, the boat got onto full power and full speed ahead: it was just like a great, white cloud behind us, with the wash of the propellors. I kept looking for the White Cliffs of Dover. I'd heard about people feeling good at seeing the White Cliffs of Dover; I was thinking about them, just on leaving. It was a very pleasant boat ride, I enjoyed it. Lots of people were sick. I wasn't 'cos I'd been used to boats.

We arrived at a place called Dieppe. I got our two cases and then I didn't have a clue what was going to happen exactly. There was nobody to organise us. All I could do was follow the rest of the gang we were travelling with. My cases were loaded down to the gunnels. There was about a quarter of a hundred-weight in each. But, as I came down the gangway, there was a porter there, bald head, short and stubby, full of smiles and very energetic. I gave him half-a-crown and I told him I was going to Paris. He seemed to understand me. He got me and Marie a lovely seat in the train, all on our own, and as he put the cases up top, I said a sort-of 'Cheer-io' to him. We waited in the station for about ten minutes then it pulled out and headed for Paris.

There was a funny thing: we went through a level crossing a few minutes after leaving the station and who should I see out of lots of people, but our porter! He recognised me, and I waved to him like fire. He waved back. I was pleased. I'd made my first friend in France, although we could hardly speak a word. If all Frenchmen were like that, well, I wouldn't mind to go to France to live.

We arrived at some station in Paris. Things were a bit chaotic there. It was something that nobody had told us about. We had to get a taxi to another, bigger station. I had no French money on me, neither did anybody else. The taxi driver said: "Two half-crowns." I was lucky, I had two more. We went all over

*see Part I

Paris, it seemed to me, anyhow. I knew we were pushing it with time to get the other train. I arrived at this big station. There were crowds of people everywhere, just like a swarm of bees. I tried to talk to different people, just hoping somebody might have spoken English. No such luck. In the end I saw a man there in uniform, not from the travel agent people. I asked him where the train for Rome was; he pointed to the platform. Marie was coming behind me and I was carrying these two hefty great cases. But things weren't how they should be, I was playing hell about it. I got to this train. Marie said: "Are you sure this is the right one?" Well, I can tell you now, if it was going to Russia or China I'd have still jumped on. I was knackered out. We jumped on.

Within no more than about four seconds, the train pulled out. We'd just made it by the skin of our teeth. It was a right hell of a job to get a seat. I didn't know the system they'd got in France, but people would shake their head and say I couldn't come there. Then a nice French guard came along the train and he sort-of made meanings that there was a seat further down the train. I don't think the people wanted us to come in the carriage, but he insisted and put our cases all up and I gave him another half-a-crown.

I didn't sleep again very much that night. I suppose I was like a child waiting for Father Christmas to come on Christmas Day. You imagine big things; you think you're in ravines and going through great, giant tunnels. I just imagined all this. In the morning it was better, when day-light came. The first thing I noticed, there were no hedgerows. I noticed all the roofs of the houses (this was in Italy) were in red pottery-type tiles; rows of grape vines. It was a hell of a long, old journey. But things were going to warm up a little bit as the trip went on.

I remember, about four o'clock in the afternoon, we were heading near Rome. Different people kept moving in and out of our carriage; then there were three men on Marie's side and maybe four or five on the other. They all looked peculiar to me; when the tallest man came in he dropped his attaché case down, opened it right in front of me and made it very easy for me to see inside it. He had a gun there and, by God, the barrel looked to me like a six inch water pipe! It really made me tremble. I whispered in my wife's ear: "Look, they're going to shoot us, but we've no brass on us, no tin, no money." And she said: "Don't be afraid." But the sweat was pouring off me and I had this big overcoat on and I thought: 'Well, shall I take it off?' and I was afraid to move. I've never been so frightened. There must have been danger of some description. In the end this bloke started asking questions. I said to Marie: "You just tell these chaps I'm just a common old farm labourer and I've worked very hard and have got just enough money to come to Italy." But the trouble was I suppose we looked rich, though we weren't; we'd dressed up smart for the journey. Anyhow, she told them, and it was a bit easier. He told Marie: "Don't worry, I'm just a Railway Detective." Well, I don't know if they have Railway Detectives or no, but my theory was that they were after our money, they were sky-hawks, and I'll always stand by it.

But we soon arrived in Rome. We changed trains for Naples. We were almost there. I was tired. I'd been travelling since Sunday night and it had now become Tuesday night. After about two hours, we arrived at Naples. Marie had recognised her family and was shouting. Her brother-in-law was there. He'd always wanted to marry my wife. He'd spoken for her. He didn't get her though. And her Dad was there and her brother and they gave me three whacking great kisses each. I've never been kissed like that before in my life! I didn't realise it was their custom and it wasn't very nice seeing fellahs with big, thick beards.

We hopped into a little car and drove on to a village that I'll call San Giovanni. They were chittering away like a cage full of budgies. I just let 'em go, let 'em enjoy themselves. I was so pleased to see Marie there, with her brother that she'd told me a lot about.

There was only one thing that was on my mind: Mount Vesuvius. I asked Marie where it was. She said: "It's on the right hand side, 'cos we're heading towards Caserta." I didn't see it because it was a darkish evening. But who was worried? We were in this land of Italy now. I was really there.

And the whole family was out there; must have been maybe thirty. It was a great thing to see this girl come home; she walked on, she was the star of the stage. And everybody forgot me; I was humping two great cases, and they walked on. I remember we had to go through a bit of a courtyard to get upstairs. And they were walking ahead of me and I remember her sister or somebody says: "Eduardo, Eduardo" (I realised this was my name). And they realised just what they were doing; it was bad manners, and they all turned round and came back and picked up the cases, and I walked along with my wife.

We had soup that night. I'm not much for these foreign dishes, so I didn't have much, and the bread was so coarse and tasted different from our bread. I just couldn't face it. There was a big box of grapes there, and I had a few grapes.

I remember, her dad and I, we walked down to the village. It was like one of those great Westerns; everybody came out to look at me. 'What is this guy, what is he?'

I retired to bed, but not to get a good night's sleep. Every hour it seemed all the bells in the church began to toll, whether it was to tell the time or ringing some religious message I don't know. In the morning I could look around. I'd wound up in a place where no foreigners had ever been. I was surrounded by mountains. It was as if some giant bulldozer had been through a piece of land and pushed up two giant furrows, and we were in the middle of it. There was snow on top on one side, even in September. The mountains came right down to our backdoor, and the sun shone like he'd never shone before.

They were at least fifty years behind time, behind us at home in Great Britain. The majority had wells and there was no mains water, but how clever they were! We always used to have to fetch our water in buckets; the well for our house was about thirty yards away from the house; but they put their pails onto a hook, they pulled a rope, and a ginny wheel slid along a metal bar; when it got to the end of the bar it would be over the top of the well, and then the pail would sink way, way down, about fifty or sixty foot; they'd pull it up, and pull the water right into their own houses. All the wells were stoned up inside and nicely kept; they're like museum pieces almost, with the stonework around them. They were still sawing timber with pit saws; my granfer had told me about things like that. They were still ploughing the land with oxen! There were two white ones in the village and they would plough beautifully. Donkeys and carts, horses and what we would call traps or jingles, of all descriptions. They never had giant great cart horses like at home; the horses were a little bit lighter than that. I was just in dreamland.

If I could only have spoken to them I could have helped them, to make life easier for them. And there were ideas they had there that I could have brought back to this country, to make life a lot easier for us people home here. Well, some I did: a little squeezy bulb to start off a syphon, knives with serrated edges at the end of the blade for sawing with, and the way they made a bit of cement in a sump, rather than on a board, so they could throw in the cement and all the water together and mix it up quickly.

I tried not to miss anything as I walked around that village, in the building line, in the agricultural line, and everything. I suppose really it was better than reading any books ever in the world.

I know we all went to Naples. Naples with trams still running. I know we were on a bus and it broke down going up a hill and we all got on another and some jumped up on top. That's exactly like at home; you broke the rules a bit, but you didn't leave anybody behind. Things like that made me laugh on the holiday.

I noticed a lot of boats were different and their method of fishing and the fish out there were a lot different from what they were at home. Naples Bay was flat, not like home at the Celtic Sea. Its cliffs weren't as high and rough and rugged, but it was a nice place just to relax.

The next place I went to that first time was a place called Monte Cassino. Marie's brother and brother-in-law came with me. I really wanted to go there. I felt I knew about the monastery because I'd worked with several men that had been there in that campaign and told me all about it. As I drove up those windy old roads, up to the top, everything that they had told about the war there came to me, as if from a lighthouse. It flashed up great beams and guided my thoughts right to the monastery. I was really impressed by the building, how it got smashed down during the war and how they reinstated it.*

* Edward went on several more visits to Italy and on one, with his friend Richard and their Italian wives, he made a pilgrimage to the English Cemetery at Monte Cassino. Christopher was also taken on two of these journeys.

I noticed so much in San Giovanni. There were no washing machines; the women used to go down to a stream and wash the clothes on the stones. They'd come back with great bundles of clothes on top of their heads, like they do in Africa. I'd never seen bread cooked like it in my life. Marie even made some cakes and put them in the clome oven. Everybody's got a verandah out there. I was looking out from my bedroom's verandah and I heard something: 'Click-click'. I came into the bedroom. There was Granny ironing with a charcoal iron! Charcoal inside the iron! They had a bottled gas stove for heating the water. They had mains sewerage; they had electric light in the village; but other than that things were very primitive. Their streets were laid out beautifully, all cobbled; the roofs seemed to hang over the streets, like kale leaves in a row.

I also noticed that the people were like the people home here in Cornwall. They were closely knitted together. They were all relations. Everybody was dedicated to the Church. It was a surprise when they heard I was a Protestant. They hadn't known of it. But I was a man of the Lord the same as they were, that was all that mattered.

People used to *teal* the gardens at our back door; they were like big allotments; *tealed* them right to the top. There wasn't a little bit of ground wasted anywhere.

I also noticed the priests had great influence over them, so I did not expect them to be as superstitious as we are in Cornwall. Once Marie's mother was taken ill. Oh! She was bad. They didn't want anybody to know too much about it — they were a respectable family, and this old farmer came and I said to my wife: "What's up here, what's all this secrecy about?" "Well, look," she said: "Mother think that someone's put a curse on her and this farmer who's come up will take away the curse from her." I wanted to laugh, because I wasn't too religious at that stage. But I got taken ill. I had heart trouble and diarrhoea and I lay in bed and I thought: 'Boy, you'll not make it back to Cornwall. Somebody's put the mockers on me.' I really did. And I asked Marie to get the farmer for me. I thought I was going to kick the bucket. Marie says: "Do you want to go through with this ceremony?" And I said: "Yes, I do." I sat on a chair and I held a big, silver cross in my hand. He read from a

Bible or a book in *I-talian* and he said: "If this cross start jumping in your hand, or vibrating, you're possessed by the Devil." And he had some water in a bottle and he made a cross on my forehead and he read on and on, and I felt great. And in the end I sort-of smiled and he looked at me and he said (or must have said): "Do you feel anything, any vibrations?" And I said: "No, none at all." Anyhow, I knew I was all right.

When you're away on holiday, you send cards home to people. I'd got Mother to write out the words before I went, to all my special friends. But I had to write to my father; he's the only living person who can understand my writing, 'cos I don't spell properly. He can sort-of look at it and guess what I'm trying to say and, in the end, he gets a pen and ink and re-writes the letter. Marie knew by this time, and filled up all the travel forms. So that's what I did in Italy as regards writing.

The worst part of a holiday is the leaving. Everybody came to Naples to see us off that morning. It was one of the hardest goings away we ever had. They even wanted me to come there and live; that's how much they wanted Marie home. But it couldn't be that way. I cried my eyes out. But in the end the electric train pulled away; we waved furiously and furiously. Marie cried for about twenty minutes, then all was forgotten: we'd left Naples behind and she talked of her son and her mama home in England and she said: "Well, I'm lucky, I've got two mamas: one in Italy and one in Cornwall, and they both love me the same."

It was a lot easier than going. We changed at Rome (*Roma!*) and headed for Paris. I found another half-a-crown. We still had to have a taxi.

CHAPTER 5

Heading Home, Westwards

WELL, THERE WERE no wars on or anything, and I'd only been away for three weeks, but believe me I got as much thrill as anybody to see our shores. It was lovely when the boat docked and I stepped on our soil once more, and soon we were heading home, westwards.

That's some feeling! Cornishmen, you're never home until you've gone over the Tamar; that's Brunel's Bridge. You know you're home then, you're nearly there. You get the smell of the sea and feel that Atlantic wind blowing in your face.

There Christopher was waiting and Grannie, or Mama Prynn. Marie picked her son up, and loved him. He loved his mama.

The first thing, when we arrived at St Merryn, we had a cup-of-tea. Everybody was really glad to see us home. I got my own car and I drove down to Harlyn Beach and just walked along the beach for a few minutes, and came home. Mother had got a dinner waiting for us. Oh! It was so good to have lovely food once more; splitters*, yeast buns and saffron cake. Oh! My mother really laid it on for me. We'd brought all different things; wine, salami, and other *I-talian* goods. My mother loved it. We talked of Italy; the stories I've told you now, I've often repeated these in tea huts and different places.

I was twenty-one years of age when I came back from Italy, and in the next couple of years I started to work in the construction business. I had lots of jobs: you might join a job when it was almost completed and you might only have a couple of months' work and then have to leave and go to another site. The boss had to give a week's notice, but if he gave it on a Monday some chaps wouldn't work as hard, so he'd tell you half-past-two of a Friday. You might think it's a bit cruel. Not really, because it can work both ways. It's nice to give your boss notice at half-

* splits, the proper bread for jam and cream

past-two as well. Some chaps used to get great pleasure out of it. There were no unions in those days. I think it was a good thing for the construction business. It's nice to have men moving around. To have the same old job, it's like *tealing* the same old crop in the same old field, after a few years it wouldn't grow nothing. I can't say all men. Some men work for companies for a lifetime, but it's nice to have some fresh men coming all the time, and that's how it was in the building business.

And here, in Cornwall, you'd get to know everybody. We'd travel great distances to work. It could be thirty or forty miles, so you got to know virtually from Land's End to the Tamar, right up as far as Bude.

Discipline was always very strict on sites. Foremen in those days held a reputation throughout Cornwall (and throughout Great Britain). Lots of foremen had a system of using what I'd called a 'weakener'. If you knew that I couldn't read or write and you wrote something on a piece of paper and waited your chance until there were a lot of people around and then gave it to me and said: "Ed, read that . . . look at that and read that a minute," and asked me all the questions, well, that would be a weakener to me. Sometimes a man would break up and couldn't go through with it. He'd give his notice in and get another job. The person that could beat the weakener system would generally come right out on top in the end.

Also, on building sites, you soon made friends. You could come on a site, a total stranger from the end of Great Britain: if you'd no dinner packed for you, everybody would share out their food and get you going and fix you up with digs; everybody helped one another. Sometimes, some wives might not be the best of cooks, and another chap in the tea hut would say: "Here, try a bit of this sponge." And that chap liked it very much and from then onward the other chap's wife would make him a bit of sponge specially, as long as he stayed on the job.

You all worked happily. When I was in the construction business, we never used to try and make a job last. We always wanted to get on with it. We always got great pleasure, all of us, in getting on with the job. It was a marvellous atmosphere.

At St Mawgan, with a Devon Company called Dudley Coles of Plymouth, our foreman was called Mr Crewe. Mr Crewe was well known. He was really one of the hardest masters I'd ever worked for. I know, the first day I was there and we had crib. It was only ten minutes. I didn't finish drinking my tea up exactly and everybody rushed out the tea hut. One of the other chaps warned me: "Ed," he said: "If you're last out for a week, you'll get the sack." 'Cos the office was always overlooking the tea hut. I soon learnt the lesson. I didn't stay a second after the whistle went. I was right on.

I had a job there as a carpenter's mate. I was lucky. I just bumped into it. I soon learnt how to measure. I could guess the last little bit, if it got down to anything fine. The carpenter liked me; I worked hard for him and did everything he wanted. People could never believe the speed we'd work, 'cos we got pleasure in working. It was fun to us.

The carpenter said to me one day: "Ed," he says: "I'm going to leave. Me and another carpenter, and we want a mate to come with us. Will you come?" I wasn't all that keen. I'd never left Marie before. I said: "I'll have to ask Marie." "Well," he said: "tell you what, the wages will be twice as much as what you're getting." I told Marie about it. I talked her into letting me go.

We were only going up to a place called Brent Tor, near Mary Tavy, to work on a reservoir. We didn't tell Mr Crewe that we were going until half-past-two on the Friday. They went down and gave in their notice and I went down as well. I got on well with Mr Crewe. He said: "I thought you would be going, Ed, with them." He said: "You're doing a silly thing. You ought to stay with me." "No," I said: "I'm going." "All right," he said: "that's it, but if you ever want a job, you can come back with me."

Well, it came we started on the new job. Marie cried her eyes out, and Mother; they were at the front door when the car came with the other two carpenters for us to head up to Brent Tor. It was only about a two-and-a-half hour journey and we were soon there. My job was to be cook.

Well, I can tell you, I couldn't cook a thing, never, 'cos Mother and Marie did everything for me. In my spare time, I had to help the carpenters. The first morning I made a terrible mess of frying the eggs. They all stuck in the pan. I've never worked out to this day what happened. I couldn't move them and there was smoke everywhere. I tried to keep the caravan as clean as I could. I don't like smells or anything like that. They used to grumble and say: "You's all the time in the caravan." But by the time I'd washed up all the dishes and cups! I got to know how ladies work round that stove. One night the carpenters came in and they couldn't eat their tea. One went off to Tavistock and came back with fish-and-chips for him and his mate. Well, that was soul destroying. I'd almost had enough. I came home that weekend. Poor old Marie wasn't too good. I went back, I didn't really want to, but I had to go back. That Monday I cooked the tea again and they really grumbled. On the Tuesday morning, about nine o'clock, I was outside the caravan and there were one or two other chaps around and there was a lovely great seagull flying overhead, a long way up, and I said to a man from Barnstaple: "Which way is that seagull heading?" "Ed," he said: "he's heading due West." I knew he was heading straight back over Trevose Head. I said: "Yes, and I'm going with 'un." I went in and gave my notice and that was it. I think the carpenters were glad in a sense. I was all right for work, but no good as a cook!

I caught the train back home and next morning I jumped on Dudley Coles' bus. Everybody on the bus said: "My God Almighty, Ed, you ain't coming back again?" I said: "Yes, I am." Because it was the only job around at that time with good pay.

Everybody else went on to work. I waited outside Mr Crewe's office. He drove down the road, he walked down the path, he hardly ever looked at me. He didn't even speak to me. He went in his office. It was always customary to knock at Mr Crewe's office. You never ever went in unless you knocked. It was a sacking offence. I knocked on the door and he didn't answer. I knocked twice; he didn't answer. I knocked once more. He said: "Come in." He's a tall man with a bald head, with glasses. He had a system, when he was sitting down, of keeping his head down and looking over the top of his glasses. He said: "What do you want?" I said: "I want to know if there's a chance of a start again." He said: "I knew it wouldn't work out, up there. I knew you did the wrong thing." In a very wild voice, he said: "Yes, you can." I was going to see the ganger, to see what I had to do. Mr Crew said: "No, I'll put you on some work. Go down to the store and get a pick and shovel." He had a big trench to dig, near his office. He said: "Right! You start digging there." That was putting me on a weakener. Well, they all thought I'd crack in the end, especially outside the Boss's office, digging, digging. It lasted for about four or five weeks. It didn't matter to me, digging. He just wasn't going to weaken me. I got over it and I was delighted. Then he put me on with another carpenter. And I was happy. I stayed there for a long time.

CHAPTER 6

A Night Out

I TOLD YOU MARIE wasn't too well. Now I came home one night from St Mawgan after she'd been to hospital, and Mother said: "Marie's up bed and she's very ill and she's got TB, and things isn't too good." I said: "Mother, I thought people go to hospital with TB?" Well, in this case, they decided that Marie could stay home. I think she was down to maybe five stone, 'cos normally she was ten stone. She was half her weight. She could hardly talk. She never had any breath at all. I came by the side of the bed and I caught hold her hand and told her: "Never mind," I said: "you'll pull through." And she just smiled. I know, my mother nursed her. When Mother used to bake cakes in the oven, and saffron buns and pasties and stuff, she used to cart them up the stairs on a tray and show Marie what was going on down in the kitchen. She wanted her to share the atmosphere with her. Mother often used to come up, because it was summer time, and smooth her brow with water, wash her hands. And the village people would ask for her. If you're bad in a village like ours, everybody comes to your rescue. They all sent flowers, and everybody was fantastic. I used to come to bed early, with Marie. She was pretty special to me, I can tell you. She really was. But slowly she began to pick up. It lasted maybe eight or nine months while she stayed a-bed, but slowly she got really better. Then there was big excitement because the doctor said she could come down next week. I told everybody in the village. They were all thrilled because they knew she had made it. She'd pulled through. Marie gave Mother and me and Father a surprise one night: she came downstairs before she should have. That was really some moment.

When Marie was taken ill we had to put Christopher in a convent school at Bodmin. And I used to go up and fetch him every weekend, but now his mum was better he no longer had to go to that school and he could come home and go to our village school, where Charley Harvey* was the School Teacher. So we were all pretty happy once more at No 8 Trevithick.

The next thing, one day Mr Crewe called me in his office. By this time I was off the weakener. I was working with the carpenter. He said: "Ed, I want you to go with Mark; I want you to go to Bideford and build an ROC post." That's an underground building. I said: "How long for?" "Oh, just a week," he says. This is another trick in the building business. If you told a man the truth, he would never go. If you want him to go for say three months, you say 'a week'. If you want him to go for three weeks you say 'well, just one day'. He said 'a week'. Well, I didn't think that was too bad. So I accepted.

Well, we set off for Bideford. We really worked the clock around, from eight o'clock in the morning until eight in the evening. It was really big wages, I can tell you. We worked hard. We had one labourer recruited from up there called Reggie. We stayed at a little house right touching the site, with Harold Radford and his wife. We were there I should estimate about three or four weeks. We really worked hard. Marie used to ring me every night. I couldn't ring her because there were no call boxes around. She used to ring me at Harold's house. They took other visitors as well. They had about four or five bedrooms. It was a big house, but the telephone was in the most damned silliest place a telephone could ever be: it was in the front room. I had to tell Marie to make it brief. I said: "When you 'phone me, just make it brief, 'cos it annoys the others when the television's going." "All right," she says. Well, we were really coining the money in. We'd only been about halfway through this job at this time and Mark, the carpenter, said to me one night: "Ed," he says: "let's give ourselves a little treat and have a night out." Well, I couldn't see no harm in it. I said: "All right." We left work early and changed up. I didn't have my best clothes, but good clothes with me. I told Harold if Marie should ring (this was wicked of me and I feel ashamed to tell you) to say that we'd got trouble on the site and we would be working very late. "All right," he says. Well, off we go to Bideford. We really had a good look around. I remember, the record at that time was

*see Part I

Elvis Presley's 'Running Bear' (or something like that). They were playing it in this sort-of dance room place. It was good music and we got almost drunk. We came home about twelve o'clock. I had the feeling all the time I was in trouble with Marie. You can sense when there's trouble around. Harold came out as we drove in. "Edward," he says: "I don't think things are too good with you and Marie." I said: "What's wrong?" He says: "She's rung here three or four times," he said: "and I've told her you've been working up on the site." "Oh! My God!" I says. Well, we went in and just watched the television with the sitting room full of people. As sure as God made little apples, that telephone rang again. I was sweating. Harold answered it. He said: "It's for you, Ed." This was Marie. I said: "Hello, My Love!" She said: "Don't you 'hello' me." I said: "I've been up working." And all the guests knew full well I hadn't been up working. She said: "You've been out, I can feel it." "No, dear." She said: "You've got to give up that job and come right home." And I said: "Yes, dear." And this is all I could say. And if you only knew Marie, that was like a weakener too in a sense, because it made her more furious. 'Cos I couldn't tell her, I couldn't tell any lies, not too much in front of everybody, and it made it worse. It made Marie so furious!

When I got home at the week-end, she'd cooled down a bit. I told her I'd look for another job. I swore to Marie under oath that there was no women involved at all. She accepted it, but I promised her that if I did have to stay there much longer, that I'd look for another job. We went back for about a fortnight. Then one day Harold came up: "Mark," he said: "there's a 'phone call for you, from St Mawgan." When Mark returned: "Ed," he said: "we've got to work this week-end and that's it. We'm heading back. We got to go back home." "Yippee," I said: "this is just the job." We went back to Mr Crewe's then, and all was happy.

CHAPTER 7

Digger Driver

IN MY SPARE TIME home here I used to do a bit of boating from On-John's Cove. I couldn't get there much because I was always working, every minute the Lord gave me. But the job was nearly finished at St Mawgan and one of the chaps organised another job for about eight of us at English China Clays. I only stayed there maybe nine months and we were pick and shovelling and digging. It was a happy company. Lots of men in the English China Clays have worked there a lifetime. They knew nothing different. We worked on the building site, not in the clay pits. But they're like one great, big family. It must be one of the best companies in Great Britain, really fantastic. But it was a long way to go on the old lorry every day.

It seemed to be a set pattern for me in life that I didn't have too much control over the things that happened. It was just what happened to me. I was over at St Columb one night, and a chap offered me a job with a lot more money, putting roofs on hangars at St Mawgan. I went there, and I worked for about six weeks. I used to ride my bike to work; that was a twenty-five mile round trip. You may think: 'Why didn't you do that with a car?' Well, I always wanted to give Marie everything; if I could save a few pounds somewhere I did. It used to take me two hours to get there, and two hours to get home, but I didn't mind that, 'cos it was that extra for Marie. She always worked as well, of course.

I must point this out to you now: a firm is (doesn't matter if it's a small firm of just two or three of you, or a firm of thousands) but a firm is only as good as its bosses are. Management; you call it that if you want to, I call 'em bosses; that's the top man, No. 1 Boss, right down the line. With bad bosses, it can be nothing short of hell to work for and I can tell you I didn't like working for anybody that couldn't organise. I liked working for the most efficient companies there ever were. The tops for me, in management, 'cos it makes it easy for everybody around, if things are organised right.

Then I went to see a new foreman at Costain's and I got a job with them again, to work as a second man with an excavator. I'll call them diggers. Second man for one of those diggers, a banksman they called them. I had several weeks at that.

One day, I heard a rumour that there was to be another digger. I hadn't been doing any driving for a few years, but I had done a lot at the quarry with mechanical shovels and I wanted to get one. I went to the office because there was keen competition to get it, and I asked for the job. The foreman was called Charley Lakey. Charley said: "Can you drive one, Ed?" "Yes," I said: "but not this sort that you're having." "That's fair enough, Ed," he said: "you've got the job." I know, within a day or two the digger came. Now I'd better tell you this: when most of you see these diggers and chaps driving them, it means absolutely nothing to you, and you think it's just another job for the bloke that drives it around. Well, you know, if you were a girl, you most probably had a pram and that was your most treasured possession; it was a toy. And you boys, if you had a toy at Christmas that you worshipped, it was always in your mind; well, that is what an earth-moving digger is like to a digger-driver. It's something very, very special; you feel part of it: it's the power. But now my big chance had come. I was driving. I mastered the job like a shot. There weren't too many diggers in action in those day and the chaps that drove them, they thought they were tin gods: by that I mean they weren't perhaps as good as they thought! But I'd done all the digging with pick and shovel by hand; I knew what that was about: donkey work. And now I was given the mechanical digger, I was going to eliminate the hardest work for every labourer on the site; which I did do.

Things were going well for me. I had a couple of years like that. And, around here, in the village, seasons came and seasons went. A lot more people, visitors around by that time. Almost everybody had got cars.

The site was soon to finish and the digger was going. The foreman said: "Ed, they want you to go to Plymouth and work this digger." I said: "Will I get overtime and everything?"

"Yes," he says: "you will." Well, I told Marie I was going and just at that time her sister died in Italy, but I had to go. I did wicked things to Marie really. The job came first, before Marie. I went a day or two after she had the news.

It took me a day to drive the digger to Plymouth. I worked long hours at Plymouth. I was out at a place called Bickleigh. I had lodgings right near the site and, to begin with, I slept in the tea hut every Friday night. I didn't go to my digs, I used to sleep on top of the table in the tea hut, to save a bit of money. It was winter when I went there: 1962, one hard winter. I used to work late, with lights, digging trenches and stuff. In the evening, I used to have my tea and come back. I used to put the digger in the old drill shed and do my maintenance on it. I never got paid for that. I used to stay there some nights until twelve o'clock, polishing and looking after my digger. That was part of my life; you'll never understand it, but I loved that digger so much.

The Army was still at Bickleigh and I used to see them training there, on the assault course. I used to see them drilling in the morning. I think I could have coped with it all right. It didn't put me off the Army, though I never went, but I could have coped with it*. I think I would have liked the discipline and the way, I suppose you'd call the sergeant, or somebody, used to shout on the men in the mornings when they were walking by. I think I'd have liked all that stuff.

But Marie didn't like this lot, down in Cornwall. She thought she'd move up with me. You remember that policeman that lived next-door, that drove me to my wedding? We keep in contact around here, with everybody; we always know where everyone lives. I knew where the policeman lived and I went to see him and asked him if we could fix me up with a flat. He had a friend that fixed me up with a flat, in St Jude's. Marie joined me. She got a job at Bush-Rank Radio Station, making radios and stuff. Well, I can tell you, it was the happiest of all the things in my life, 'cos we'd lived home all the time with Mother, as Marie didn't want to leave there. It was the first time I'd ever lived on my own, with Marie. It was out of this world. The ultimate happiness with her. I used to start some mornings at five o'clock and didn't get home until half-past-eight. Marie

---

*Edward was not accepted for National Service — see Part I

would get tea and then I would help her to thread up; she taught me how to put together lots of these things for radios and electronics stuff, and I used to help her to thread different things on to wires and other little jobs. And last thing, about half-past-ten, I used to walk down to the Barbican and see the water. If you're a Cornishman, if you can see the water, well, once a week, you're happy. Don't matter where it's to in the world, you know that would lead you home, if need be.

We had the downstairs flat, and there was an upstairs flat. There was a woman there, I forget her name, and she had a daughter, Betty, that was married to a matelo at that time and he went abroad on a ship and she was at home on her own. Well, I suppose we'd call her a bit of a fly-by-night, perhaps. She was out late hours, came home one o'clock. Marie used to say to me: "Did you hear Betty come in last night?" "No," I'd say: "I ain't interested." Marie knew what she was about. Betty often used to come down and talk to me. In the morning, when I'd get the car, Marie would still be doing her little jobs in the flat perhaps; I'd get the car and wait outside the flat: Betty would nip out and jump in the front seat. Marie would come out and get in the back. Well, I can tell you straight, I never took any notice of it. I didn't care who rode in the front or who rode in the back. Marie pointed it out one night to me. She said: "I don't like this damn Betty." She said: "She's taking over with you."

Well, I can tell you I wasn't interested; all I thought about was Marie, Christopher and my digger. I wasn't interested in anybody else. But Marie started playing up a little bit. She wanted to go home. She said she didn't like the flat. She was home-sick for Mother and wanted to go home to Cornwall. She told Betty one night, when we were down in the kitchen: "I'm thinking that I'm going home." "Well," she said: "Marie, if you do, Edward can come and lodge with us, we've got a spare room." Marie soon gave up the idea about coming home! I said: "Are you going home?" She said: "No, not unless you come with me." Under no circumstances was Marie going to leave me behind with Betty! Well, I've no doubt there would have been trouble.

I promised Marie if another job turned up I would accept it. I came home one week-end and there was a new firm started, called Mid-Cornwall Contractors, owned by Boss Crotty. I'd seen him and known him when I'd worked for Costain's back at St Mawgan. I promised Marie I'd go that way and look in to see what he said, and driving back to Plymouth on that Sunday night, about seven o'clock, I called at Mid-Cornwall Contractors' depot and there was Boss Crotty, serving petrol on the forecourt. I had some petrol and I said: "Boss, is there any chance of a job?" He said: "You work for Costain's don't you?" I said: "Yes, on the digger." "Yes," he said: "you can start tomorrow, if you want to." "No," I said: "not tomorrow, I've got to give a week's notice." Marie was thrilled, because we didn't have to go back there any more, for no more than the last week.

On that Monday morning I told Ivor, the ganger, and I told Stan Dicks, the foreman; and then Mr Whittle, the site agent, sent for me. He said: "Why are you going home, Ed?" I said: "Marie don't like the flat and she want to go home." He said: "Ed, we'll find another flat for you and get something special and keep you here." "No," I said: "Mr Whittle, I've got to go."

I did love it up there, with the Plymouth people. It was a fantastic site. I got on so well. I loved my digger. I loved everything about it there at Bickleigh, just on the edge of Dartmoor. But there, I had to go. It was sad to leave. I came up that Friday, the last afternoon. I said "Cheer-io" to all the guys there. Everybody knew me, I knew everybody else. I said "Cheer-io" to Ivor. I might as well tell you, I was crying. I couldn't say 'Cheerio' to Stan Dicks and I never said 'Cheerio' to Mr Whittle. I just walked away from the site and took one last look at my digger and felt it was the end of the world. I really did love it at Plymouth, and all the people there, there was so much happiness, no bickering, no falling out. What fun we had! There was never a dull moment.

But before I leave Bickleigh, I'd better tell you about my reading and writing. It was all right, I didn't have to bother with it, 'cos gangers did all the filling out of the time sheets. I never came unstuck with that, there. I always had a ganger with me to do the measuring and setting everything out. I just worked the digger. I knew how to take the levels off. If they said they wanted to take off six foot of earth here or so deep, I could take it off just like a man slicing off bacon with a bacon machine.

So we packed up all our cases at the flat and drove back over the Tamar and back home to Cornwall once more.

CHAPTER 8

Boss Crotty

WELL, HOME TO CORNWALL. I'd left Richard Costain's behind. They were happy times, especially when Marie and I were living in the flat. But once more, we had to come back home and live with my parents. I didn't like it, but Marie got on so well with Mother and Father, and they held all the power over me; so long as they were happy, who was worried? I had happiness at work, that was the real happiness that I had. But soon I was going to start at Mid-Cornwall Contractors.

There's always one thing that bothers you when you change jobs: your old boss might think the world of you, and all your mates, but on the next job you could be nothing and get the sack within a week or two. It's always nice to come on a job where nobody knows much about you and you haven't got anything to prove, even if you're just a pick-and-shovel hand. It's better that nobody knows anything about you and then you get to the top quicker. I was worried about this, starting with Mid-Cornwall Contractors.

But I think I'd better tell you a bit about my boss: he was called Hamilton Crotty. He once worked at St Lawrence's Hospital as a male nurse. He then got a filling station; his mother had a filling station, and he took it over. And then he bought a few bulldozers and diggers and started a plant hire firm. I always get a great thrill out of these sort of people. I've got my own saying: 'It takes two generations to build a castle and one silly devil can knock it down again.' But Boss Crotty built the castle in a few years, on his own. He was the type of man who, if you were out on sites, changing equipment and maybe it was raining and muddy, and he happened to come around there to see how you were getting on (it wouldn't matter if he had his blue suit on), would really come in and swing that sledge hammer and screw up bolts, or help you on another job.

1 Edward with Mules

2 Edward and Christopher

In Italy

3 Oxen Ploughing

4 Granfer outside his Local

5 Jack Prynn, Les Martin, and Mates at Wheal Path, St Merryn

6 Edward and Excavator at Virginia Clay Pits

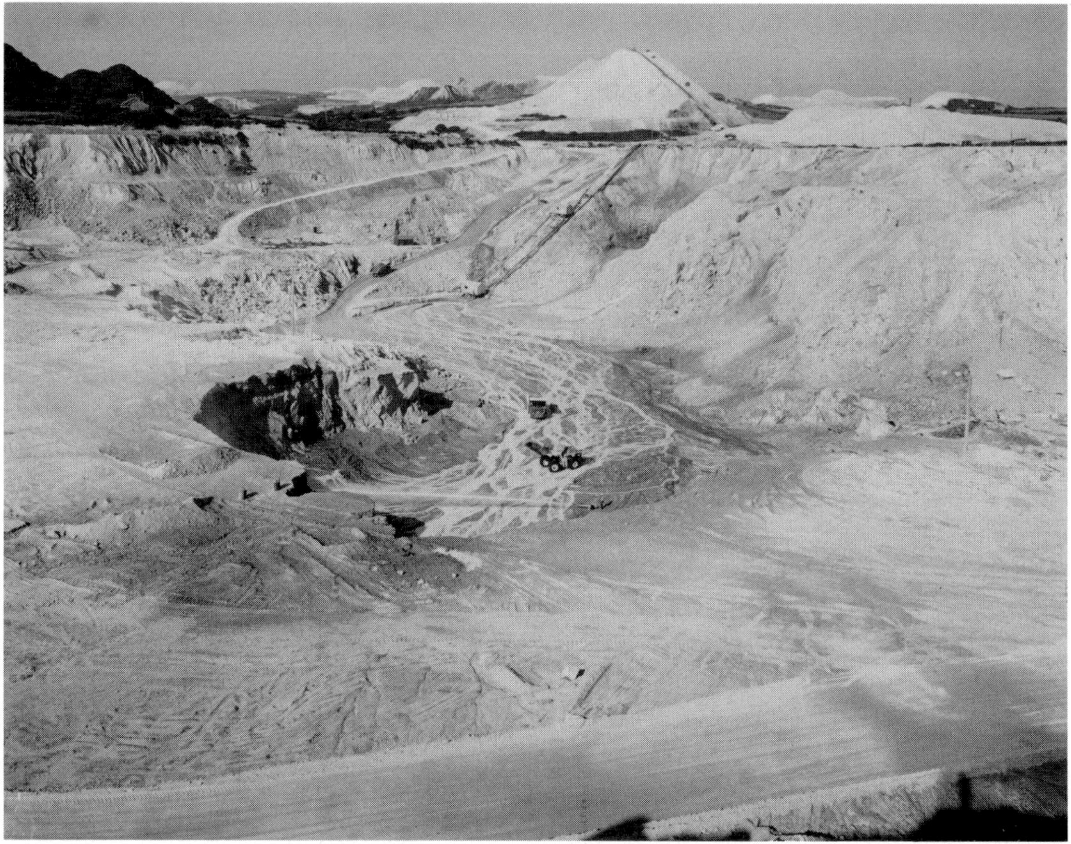

7 St Austell Clay Pit

He wasn't afraid of a bit of dirt. It's very special to workers, if management can keep close to them. I believe that is the right system. Boss Crotty always looked after all his employees. He had no-one but the best. He had no personnel manager, not in the early days; he did it all himself. He had the gift; he'd probably have made the best personnel manager for a giant company that there ever was. No one could equal Boss Crotty. In my opinion, that is the secret of all companies: the personnel manager or the man who takes on staff. That is one of the greatest skills that ever was, and nobody ever realises it. You never hear anybody mention how good their personnel manager is; and he is the key to the whole problem.

But there, I was at Mid-Cornwall Contractors, with Boss Crotty at the wheel and the best staff coming from all over Cornwall, with a young firm that was just starting. Boss Crotty, he was like the sun himself. He would generate heat wherever he was, and that was why his company had a reputation.

Well, there's something I'm going to tell you now: these next six years I worked with Boss Crotty were going to be the last six years I was ever going to work in my life. Something happened . . . so I want you to enjoy the last six years with me, and I'm going to start you off on my first day, down at Fowey with an old digger, working for the County Council. I stayed there for three weeks.

Boss Crotty sent for me back to the office. I had to report back at the garage. If you've got to go to the office, maybe your boss doesn't know it, but it frightens you up a little bit. You just wonder what's going to happen: I hadn't done anything wrong and Boss Crotty never had a reputation for sacking people, but I was nearly last in.

I went to the back yard. Boss Crotty told me he'd got another, brand new digger coming, and he would take someone on to drive mine. I really couldn't believe it! Marie had given me a new bike, but I'd never had a new car or anything else; Boss Crotty was going to put me on a brand new digger! Some drivers never get a brand new one in a lifetime, but there it was, I hadn't been there very long and I had! It was really a great thrill.

You all know, when you get a brand new car, you sort-of show it off and drive around to your neighbours, find a little excuse to go and call on somebody. Well, that's just how it was with the digger. As I was known throughout Cornwall it made me feel great!

I used to clean Boss Crotty's digger every night when I left work. It didn't matter how muddy it was; sometimes on building sites there could be mud three, four foot deep, and concrete and dust, but it never made any difference. I never refused work. (If I did, if I grumbled or groused, I would never be wanted back on the site again.) That was my thrill, to clean the digger after I left work. I didn't care how much mud they put me through or how much bramble or anything. I would paint what scratches there were. I kept the digger in tip-top condition. That was my work; I didn't want it to be broken down and have no work. I had something I loved doing. I got paid well for it, and I put the best into it.

I went to a place called St Mawgan; I've mentioned it before; where I met a great personality. On building sites, a tea-boy is a bit of a legend. A good tea-boy is the only person I know who can make a cup-of-tea for a hundred people on just one packet. Now you ask: 'Well, how on earth do he do it?' Well, I'll tell you the secret: he never chucks away his grounds, his tea leaves; he keeps them in a plastic bag or in a two-gallon pail, anything that will hold them. Keeps 'em nice and dry. And then he works with two gallon of tea leaves for every brew and just chucks away a few, adding a little bit of fresh. Bert Cook, our tea-boy, was one such chap and used to operate in this manner.

I remember one day that made me laugh; Bert had a great wrapper of bacon there, and he shouted in the tea hut (we might have been sixty or eighty men inside): "Would anyone like a fried bacon sandwich?" "Yes, please Bert, but how much?" "One-and-three." Honest, it was down right robbery. Everybody shouted and said: "No, you can keep 'em" and made rude gestures. A chap on my table, called Whacker King (a nickname) said: "God Almighty! Ed, I think that's outrageous of old Bert. He won't sell many of they." Anyhow, Bert says: "Please yourselves, I'm going to fry one myself." Bert put the frying pan on, and soon the lovely smell of bacon seemed to rumble through the room; everybody was spellbound by it. Even I, was almost tempted to have one. Whacker King, on my table, said: "Ed, I got to eat humble pie. I'm going to have a sandwich: I can't resist it." Nor could all the moaners that grumbled about the high price. Bert sold the bacon and he went on for many weeks, until they all got tired of it. He told me later: "I knew 'twould work, once I started frying, they couldn't resist it." So there you are: tea-boys like Bert, they've all got a way to lure their customers into buying some little *trinklet* or other.

CHAPTER 9

A Piece of Steel

I KNOW MARIE WAS happy with things. Things were good. We used to go to beach Sundays when I had Sundays off, 'cos I normally worked seven days a week, month in and month out, but what time there was, we used to go to beach, most probably in the evenings. When Marie came home from work, I always used to go and put the car away with her and come back arm-in-arm, and all the people in our council estate used to look out the window and say: 'Gor, what a devoted couple.' Well that's how it was. We used to hold hands, just like young, spring couples. Everything was perfect then.

In 1969 I had another new digger. It was going to be my last, but I wasn't to know it. I went to work at a site called Virginia; not Virginia in America, Virginia at St Austell Clay Works. Beautiful surroundings, right down in a valley with steep hills running right down to meet, almost; lots of trees, and a very pleasant place to work. It was nice that particular summer; there was no big overtime, it was steady going. I did a lot of fishing back at Harlyn (On-John's Cove) in the evening.

I had my digger to clean; every night I used to clean it and polish it. And it shone, just like a bit of tinsel on a Christmas tree. I got very conscious, if we were ever hammering steel and stuff with hammers; I'd always look the other way and put my hand in front of my eyes. I was very conscious of this. I know often, when I was driving home from work — perhaps something made me, or told me: 'Put your hand in front of your good eye and see how good the lazy eye is.' I used to try it, and nearly wind up in the hedge. I used to try to drive the digger sometimes, and close my good eye. I often used to swing around and thump right into a big dumper and get a 'busing from one of the drivers.

I know once, I saw a guy wearing safety goggles. I thought to myself: 'God! I must get a pair. I really must.' I rang the workshop and asked if I could have a pair. "As soon as they come, the first pair you shall have Ed."

I had a holiday in October time. I always had one ambition, to go to Manchester and watch Georgie Best play. I did go and I saw George Best. It really felt special to me to be there with all those thousands of people. I had never really been in that atmosphere in my life. I had a nice holiday in Manchester for a week, and came home, and back to work as usual.

I know there was one particular night, well actually on the 19th October, I stayed behind because the fishing was almost over, and really cleaned my old digger up, everywhere. There was not a speck of oil or dirt nowhere. It really shone like a gentleman's Rolls Royce; the headlamps, the glass, and all the scratches painted in. When I walked up from Virginney that night ('cos my van was right up the top of the pit) I kept looking behind. I was so pleased to see it sparkle like that. The higher I got, so it looked more special, like seeing some big, special ship that was going farther and farther away. I kept on looking at that glitter. Two-and-a-half hours, they were worth every bit of it; I was happy in what I'd done. If a man's happy in what he's doing, even if 'tis wrong sometimes and he isn't hurting anybody, it's better to leave 'un carry on.

It came to next morning. The wind was down to zero, dense fog. I really had a hell of a job to drive my little Mini van to work that morning. I got to the top of Melbur Pit; there I was to drive a big thirty-ton dumper down to the lower entrance. It took me almost half-an-hour to drive the big dumper down this dumper road, which was very dangerous. I had to keep the wipers going, and the lights on. I was almost afraid I was going to drive over the edge. It really was terrible. I tried to put my head out of the window, but it was hopeless. I inched my way down till I got to the bottom.

We started off work as usual. The sun began to come through about nine o'clock, and push away the old mist clouds. I decided as I were only loading two dumpers, I would change the teeth; they are teeth on the lading bucket that would rip into the rock. I changed three and I was working on the fourth one. I'd got it on, but I couldn't get the cutter pin down by just a little bit. I had a pound-and-a-half hammer and I gave it a blow on the top of the

tooth. This is high tensile steel, the tooth is. I just couldn't get
this cutter pin in. I hit it once, twice and no go. I gave it one
more blow.

Oh! My God! It was like a bit of shrapnel . . . it went right
through my good eye . . . I just fell down on my knees . . . it was
just like stuff that runned out of my nose, all slime and that. It
went all over my face. I cried like a baby.

For once in my life, I had the best job in all the world. I was
the most happy chap in the whole world. I just had everything.
I'd reached the summit. And now the Good Lord had taken me
away from it. I knew the end was up. I knew I'd be chucked out
on the scrap-heap.

One of the dumper drivers came back. He said: "What's up,
Ed?" I said: "I've run a piece of steel through my eye." "Well,"
he said: "you've got two haven't you?" "No," I said: "I ran a
meat skewer in it when I was young; I can't see nothing hardly."
He didn't know what to say.

I pulled myself together. I didn't want to show I was weak in
front of the others, but I really was. As I walked away from the
digger I could just hear the engine ticking over. That was it, for
ever, when I left Virginney Pit.

Someone drove me to St Austell Hospital. I had to lie down on a
bed. I didn't want to. I was restless. I wanted to go home. They
insisted I had to go to hospital. Nurse couldn't do anything for
me there, as it was only a Cottage Hospital. She just put a patch
over it. They informed Boss Crotty what had happened. As I
was going to City Hospital, Truro, I said: "Don't tell Marie, not
my wife, 'cos I'll be home again at three o'clock."

I know, although it was a lovely, hot, roasting day, I was just
freezing cold. They wrapped me up in blankets. Dr Rostron
checked me over and asked me where the bit of steel was. I said:
"I don't know." He X-rayed it and he said: "It's still lodged up
in your eye: quarter of an inch long and about the size of a pencil
lead." He put his hand right in front of my lazy eye and asked
me how many fingers I could see. He was only about three
inches away. I could see his hand, but when he asked one finger
or two, it was just guessing.

They took me up into a ward. Just after dinner Marie came. I
really felt sick. I'd let poor Marie down. When I started off in

life and took her to Padstow Church and married her, I wanted to give her everything, just like every other man wants to give to a woman. Now she was in lumber with me. They weren't crocodile tears, they were tears that we were together and she was going to look after me, whether I was rubbish or not rubbish.

All my mates came to see me. Douggie Duguid, he came almost every night. I got on reasonably well with the nurses. I had one little fall-out with one. Apparently, on the door, it said 'Only two visitors' and one night I think I had about ten or fifteen. That's no exaggeration. And when everybody had gone, she gave me a right roasting. I told her I couldn't see what was on the door (and if I'd seen I couldn't have read it, but I wasn't going to tell her that!) I really gave her a roasting back, but that was the worst thing I could ever do. I discovered nurses have a little way of punishing you. They go all quiet and cool. It was just like when you're on the sea; a lull before the storm; and that's what these nurses were like; made me feel I didn't know what was going to happen next.

They used to detail other patients to lead me around. Boy, wasn't I in some condition? I kidded lots of my mates that I might make it back, but I knew myself I couldn't.

CHAPTER 10

On the Scrap-Heap

BUT SOON I WAS to get discharged and sent home from the hospital. I knew there was one person that I had to go and see before I got home. Only Marie knows about this: I had to go and see Granny Taylor*. I felt that might be the only luck for me. Marie drove me to see Granny Taylor. Granny Taylor put her hands on my eyes. I felt I was privileged. She very rarely did that for anybody, but she did it for me. She said: "If the Lord wants you to get better, Edward, it will. If He won't, you'll stay as you are. I can't help you really, only the Good Lord."

I came home feeling happy after leaving Granny Taylor. She had no qualifications or nothing else, but she had something spiritually, something that no person in the world would ever put a price on.

I know Marie was to tell me in later years that they thought about removing my eye completely. She said: "I always think that Granny Taylor did you some good." I'll always believe Granny Taylor did me a lot of good, just that one visit.

When I got home, I just ran in quickly, I didn't want any one to see me. I was walking with my head upright. It hurt poor old Mother and Father to see me like this. Whenever I poured out milk into my cup, I would miss and pour the milk on the table. I know I fell down the stairs, bumping into everything; I was always falling down. I know the biggest thing that hurt me was, not the weekends, when all my mates were home; it was Monday mornings when I heard in this housing estate, maybe half-past-six, different guys starting up their cars and going to work. I couldn't go.

But a few weeks passed; I felt a bit depressed, and I decided I was going to Harlyn Beach. It frightened Marie and Mother out of their life, and Father, when I said I was going. I said: "I've got

*The faith healer — see Part I

8 Edward's Mother and Father

9 Harlyn Bay. Rough and Calm Seas

10 Launching the Padstow Lifeboat

11 Edward and Donald Dark with their Boat Susie Ann III

12 Logan Stone at Tresallyn Cross

to go." They said: "Don't fall over a cliff, be careful." I went down and I walked on Harlyn Beach. And there the beach was, nobody had been there (all the visitors had gone) and to my amazement I walked on some beautiful pieces of wreck. I almost fell over them. They were big, and right there. I tried to look across to the other side of the beach, just like I used to. I'll describe my sight, how it was: it was just as if you were driving down the motorway at night and both your brilliant headlights went and then you were only driving on sidelights. That was what it was like: I couldn't look across, never had the range. I could only see that little bit in front of me. But I've always said the sea's a magic place. I think old Harlyn Bay gave me something that day to cheer me right up. I had enough wreck to keep us going all that winter. I had a giant pile. Everywhere I walked I just fell over it, and I gathered it all together and got someone to drive my little car and get it home for me. That was fantastic.

I made several trips up and down to the hospital; kept going. Dr Rostron told Marie: "You know he'll never work again. He'll have to train for another job, maybe making baskets or something else." Well, I must tell you straight, I didn't feel like going up to London or anywhere like that. Maybe you're a bit ashamed of me. I didn't do something great, and prove myself once more. I most probably have let a lot of people down, but there: it can't be helped. It's just the way it happened. I wouldn't have minded making baskets; if it was right home here in Cornwall it would have been no problem. But two of the officers working for the blind told me there were virtually thousands making them and there didn't seem to be a market for them. I didn't want to leave Cornwall. I was 'fraid I couldn't face it; people and the education side of things. It had been easy with diggers and in the construction business; I could get by on labouring and donkey work. From now onwards if it were going to be anything, another job, it would need brains, and I didn't have them.

I just had to bear up with it and soldier on the best way I could; just hang on tight to myself. I was like a ship in a storm; so long as the hatches were battened down safe, I'd ride that storm out, that's what I planned on doing.

Marie was working; she did hotel work and then she became a nurse. We lived home here with Mother and Father; I'd earned

big wages, but now I'd just got to accept it. I was on sick pay for
those early few weeks. Boss Crotty came to see me, and his
foreman, very often. Douggie Duguid was always a regular
visitor when he was home working, and he never missed a week
but he telephoned me when he was away. We kept very close
together. Douggie talked me into coming to the firm's party.
Marie didn't want to go, but Doug said I must come, 'cos we'd
had some great fun there. I went to the party, at Newquay. I had
the feeling I was like a flag that had flown at the top and then
somebody had pulled me right down to the bottom. I didn't
belong there. I made the best of it, and I joked and laughed. I
had the feeling I was ruining the party for everybody by going,
but I put on a brave face. But why I'm telling you is this: something happened I didn't like or Boss Crotty didn't like. Unknown
to me they made a collection and, at a rough guess, I had about
fifty pounds from my mates, and they called me up on the stage
and one of the foremen gave it to me. It was a marvellous
gesture from my friends, but it hurt me, but not so much as it
hurt Boss Crotty. Boss Crotty called me to one side of the party:
"Ed," he said: "I'm very upset tonight." It ruined his party too.
Boss said: "Who organised it?" "I don't know." "Ed," he said: "I
don't ever want to see you or any of my men have gifts from
anybody." He said: "I don't like that." I didn't say to him:
'Well, I don't like it.' I said: "I'm sorry it's happened Boss."

But Boss Crotty went on and paid me for twelve months that
I never worked for the Company. It was a real embarrassment.
He was the best No 1 Boss I ever worked for. I could talk about
'un for ever and ever. He was the tops. He was the sun.

After Christmas that year, I know it was about January,
Doug Duguid rang me up one night and said: "Ed, I'm going to
Wales." Boss Crotty had a big job in Wales on the Glynneath
By-Pass. He said: "Would you like to go to Wales for a couple of
days with me? I've just got to go up and repair a machine and be
right back, staying overnight." I asked Marie if I could go.
"Yes," she said. I could go; it would do me good, she thought. I
went with Doug. I knew some of the spanners. He used to say:
"Ed, bring me a 16" (or a 6 or whatever he wanted), but I
couldn't see the numbers on the spanners, not like I used to. He
had to come to the Landrover and get all his tools. I didn't really

help Doug, but it didn't matter, he was delighted to have me there. I know I took my suit: we changed up and all the lads that were working there said we were going to have a night out for me. They were all on big money. I never drink very much: a couple of pints and I'll be on the floor if I drink the third one; but they were all tanked up with ale. We danced. It was great music; I did a bit of dancing. I know at one stage, the others were all enjoying themselves and I sat down in the room and made out to watch television; you learn to be a bit of a faker, when you lose your eye-sight, or I did. On the way back to the lodgings, we did the Padstow 'Obby 'Oss: we 'oss'd and sang at the tops of our voices. I led the procession. It's a wonder we did not get locked up by the police up there.

It was so cold that night, I wrapped up all the carpets from the floor and put them on the bed; I thought I was going to die. There was another chap I slept with (he lives just a few doors away from me now; he's got his own business and doing well; he's building a castle, but at the time he was just a driver). I put all the stuff on the bed and we laughed about it all night. He said: "Ed, I'd never believe it." I said: "Boy, we won't make it here or be alive in the morning with this cold." But there wasn't going to be so good a reception for me when I got home. I was black, my face was black. Marie was absolutely furious with me, for being so black. At that time, I didn't see her point. She loved me so much, she was afraid of my eyes and that I might have to have my eye out. With the eye gone, there'd never be any chance, because Marie believed that one day somebody would fix me up. We had some hell of a dust up. A man says things sometimes to a woman that he wished he never said. Well, this was such a situation. I said: "Pack your bags and go." It was not a weakener or anything. I wasn't trying to call her bluff. It wasn't like playing five card brag. I said: "Marie, I'm hopeless now, I'm a dead loss. You're young. Go find yourself somebody, don't stick around with me. I've had it for ever." She wouldn't go; the rows we had then, we soon made it up and it was all right.

CHAPTER 11

Feeling My Way

SUMMER CAME AROUND. I know, I used to get a lot of difficulty in going to sleep. I'd spent hours thinking about what I'd do, trying to work out how I was going to earn my living, or how things were going to work out. I was something like a clockwork train, wound up for work; when the spring had run right down, then I'd be all right.

But it came around First of May and Padstow 'Obby 'Oss Day once more. It was lovely to go to Padstow. Everybody all shouted: "Hello, Ed!" It made me feel welcome. I wasn't chucked on the scrap-heap. Maybe I was for work, but not with the people at home here, in St Merryn and Padstow. And as I had a boat with my friend Donald Dark in partnership, I spent a lot of time that first year, boating. I used to get people with good eye-sight, if they would come with me; I would row and we would go fishing. Sometimes they'd bring their children with them, maybe a bottle or two of beer, and we'd row and I'd show them all the little coves, Mother Ivey's, Big Guns, Trevone, Newtrain, Rocky Beach. I met a lot of people that summer. Douggie Duguid had a week's holiday and came over and had a week with me, fishing, too. I got by.

Well, winter came on again. I was just making the odd trip to hospital now. I made several trips to Granny Taylor. I used to feel good after I'd been to Granny Taylor. When you're crocked up like me, in the early stages, you train yourself (people that are totally blind know what I'm talking about); you learn to feel with your feet, the pavements and stuff; you don't lift your feet five mile in the sky. It's like a crane driver, lifting something very delicate; he's only got to lift it five foot, he doesn't lift it fifty foot in case anything goes wrong and it's all damaged. That's how a blind man treats his body, or his legs: you don't lift your legs too high. You learn about bushes or shrubs that are overhanging; you learn your way in through gateways. I trained myself. I thought maybe one day I'd be totally blind. In case that day ever turned up, I trained myself for it.

Around here, in this little village, there are a lot of people who'd say to be classed as a cripple you've got to be totally blind, with no arms and legs, in a wheel chair. Then they'd accept you were really crippled. (I most probably thought the same way once). But there are a lot of people who probably say they don't suppose Ed is as bad as he makes out. Well, I don't think they'd like to change places with me, and I hope in the Lord's name that they never have to.

Some, and it doesn't matter if they're rich or not rich, always wear the same sort of clothes. You get to know 'em. There's one girl here, who lives four or five doors away from me; she's got blond hair and whenever I get close to her I always notice her, no problem. Some have different sorts of dogs, and this is how you get to know them. There's another woman with an old bike that always squeaks; I can always tell when she is coming. You get to know cars, until people change them. But everybody soon learns the lesson: they always give me a couple of toots and I wave my hand. I was accused once of being a snob by a bloke (not a village man, a man who came here to retire; I met him in the pub). "Ed," he says: "I reckon you're a proper snob." I said: "Why?" He said: "I put my hand up to you for almost nine months and you never look at me or acknowledge it." One of the other men in the Pub said: "I'm sorry, Sport, Ed can't see very good, unless you blow your hooter he wouldn't know who you was." Poor chap, he felt sick. I said: "Don't worry about it."

But really I'm lucky. I've got some super lot of people that live here in Cornwall, in St Merryn and in Padstow. But if you didn't speak to me I wouldn't know who you were, I'd walk right on by you. It was terrible for my son, Christopher. A time or two he walked up and didn't speak to me, and I walked right on by, and never spoke to him. My father did it as well. My family soon learnt about that.

I know the second year came around. By this time I had had a medical and I had an industrial pension. The days rolled by. It came up about 5th June, Royal Cornwall Show Day. About eight of us went in a gang. There was a fortune teller there, a

young little gipsy maiden. The others walked on. 'Well,' I
thought, 'they don't need her, their futures are all set for them;
I'll just see what she's got to say to me.' She wanted a pound. I
said I couldn't pay her a pound. She asked me why I couldn't? I
said: "You tell me my fortune and I'll give you one good reason
why I can't pay you a pound; I'll give you fifty pence and that's it."
Decimal money had come in that spring. She told me that I'd be
reasonably well off. She told me a lot of other things that I can't
remember. It did seem to make sense. She told me there would
be another woman; I'd break my heart for her. I couldn't believe
it, because I loved Marie. That's what the gipsy told me, but it
didn't really bother me, and I never thought any more about it.

I know I went to a lot of different sorts of faith healers. When
you're crocked up, you try everybody and I suppose I've tried
almost everything. I went to a lot of spiritual meetings. I also
met another medium, that told me she couldn't cure me (she was
a faith healer, but very psychic). She also told me that help would
come in a mysterious way. It would be a lot of advantage to me.

CHAPTER 12

Moorfields

PROBABLY THE NEXT summer, I met a young boy on the
beach. He spoke posh. I asked him where he came from and he
told me he came from Henley. I said: "Can you row?" He said:
"Yes, I row at Eton." I said: "Well, I've got a boat, would you
like to have a row?" He must have been about thirteen, maybe
fourteen at that time.

We took the old wood boat out and boy, couldn't this boy
row! Row; we pulled the boat everywhere! For a week or a
fortnight he came fishing. He loved the water, he loved the sea;
he loved me. I remember at the end of the holiday, he asked me
back to meet his mother and father, that were staying at Harlyn
Bay. When I went, I met his dad. He told me that he was an eye
surgeon from London, at Moorfields Eye Hospital. He had a
look at my eye. He knew Dr Rostron. He asked me many
questions and if I'd like to go to London. He said: "Edward,
there's some new treatment that we're going to start. It's like
flashing lights. It just might help your lazy eye. Would you like
to come? It might not be any good. It may be a waste of time." I
said I would have to see what Marie says, because Marie was my
No. 1 Boss. I didn't do anything without Marie. Marie agreed
we should go.

And within a matter of maybe a week or a fortnight, we were
in London. We stayed with some people at Thurrock, or Marie
did. I was in the hospital. I know, when Marie left me at Moorfields, High Holborn, and walked away, about ten o'clock in the
morning, I was in a little room on my own, and I cried like a
baby. A man shouldn't cry, but then I couldn't help it. I was in a
big city and I didn't know anybody. And I suppose I was a bit
worried about Marie travelling around London on her own.

But nevertheless, I was happy there at High Holborn. I only
stayed at that hospital for a night or two. I went out somewhere

to a place called Highgates, an annexe to High Holborn. It may
have been two or three miles away; that's where I slept, and I
came back in to High Holborn Hospital every day. The treatment
I had was in a little room on my own, putting up on the board Es
and Ns and Ws; with my type of eye-sight they're hard to sort
out. I had to put them up on a magnetic board and then walk
back to a seat and and look through a machine and see which
way they were going. Or close my eyes and jiggle them all up
myself and then see how many I'd got right.

I also watched flashing lights and had all sorts of treatment,
watching a little spot to make this lazy eye come straight. To
everybody's amazement there, it was just like work to me; I had
a chance to get cured and I was going to put in maximum effort
for it. It was for my own good. It didn't make any difference to
the doctors, (I know it *does* make a difference to them; they do
like to see you get better,) but mainly you've got to help
yourself. I followed this treatment from about nine in the
morning until four in the afternoon. I only stopped for a few
minutes at lunch time. They'd never seen anybody work like
that or put in so much time about it. They were dumbfounded.
In the construction business, I'd been used to going without
dinner time, except for a few minutes. I only need ten minutes
for lunch, that was no problem to me. I just wanted to get
better. If it meant putting in a bit of extra time on that machine,
I'd have stayed all night.

There I was going to meet a lady that specialised, not a
doctor, but she knew a lot about eyes and testing eyes. She was
called Miss Bullock, Kathleen Bullock. I know I went on with
this game for about three or four weeks, and there wasn't much
progress, but one particular day I asked her if she could stick a
bit of plaster on my glass over the only little bit of eye I'd got,
to cover it up, just to make me look out the other side. She didn't
think it would do any damage, and she tried it. Instantly, from
the time we did it, my sight improved. In virtually seconds,
we'd got the lazy eye back to work, going as straight as possible.
Well, I cried again! Though I'm ashamed to tell you, but that's
about the last time I did cry, and Kathleen Bullock saw it. I
cried because we had achieved something. I'd made it. I'd made
the breakthrough. That's what my crying was about. My sight was

three times better than when I went there, or even more. She was so pleased and so was I.

I stayed on at Moorfields for maybe a couple of weeks, always practising with the letters on the board, rather than looking at the spot. Now that little bit of patch covering up most of the glass of my one eye made me look out around. Before, the eye was turned to one side. But it made my eye sort of look around the corner and come straight. I'd thought: 'Well, roses will go anywhere if you train 'em. If you put an obstacle in the way, they'll either climb over or get around it.' And that's how it was with this patch and my eye. I don't know if they do it now with other patients. I never asked, but it certainly worked on me.

And I'll describe my sight now. I said before it was like driving down an unlit motorway with only side lights. Now it's like driving down the motorway in daylight, but its bucketing with rain and your wipers have stopped. You just get by. It's the easiest way I can describe my sight.

CHAPTER 13

Religious Mania

I CAME HOME from London. Marie used to read every article in the papers about eyes. I still went to see Granny Taylor occasionally. I went to spiritual meetings and faith healers. I kept trying, hoping perhaps one day a miracle would happen for me. I think we all do when we're crocked up; never give up. But not giving up was more on Marie's part than mine. I was like a boxer. I knew when I was beat, but I didn't want to let Marie down. I went along with anything she suggested. You never know.

I know, one day, I met just an ordinary chap, but he'd got religion. He'd become a preacher. He'd heard about me and asked me how my sight was. I told him: "No deterioration, no better." He said: "Would you like to be cured?" I said: "I'd like to be cured more than anything in the world." He said: "Well, you come with me Sunday night and we'll see what we can do." To which I agreed. I told Marie. There was no problem. Anything to get fixed up, Marie would give it her blessing.

We set off, and went to a house, about twenty miles away. We went inside, and in the room I should say there were about fifteen ladies of all ages from about fifteen to seventy and there were three men: myself, the preacher, and a chap with a bad leg. Well, they sang a few hymns and they had discussions about religion. They told me something about being re-born, how you get a second chance in life to become a Christian. At one stage I thought it might have been some coven, as there are several of them operating in Cornwall; I didn't know exactly the lie of the land. I must confess to you I thought there might sometimes be a little bit of an orgy like, because that night, driving home, the preacher said: "Some nights we go on till two in the morning. Will it be all right if we have to stay overnight?" And I said: "Yes, that will be all right." Because I had wicked thoughts in my mind. I wasn't sure what was up! I went back again the following week. There were young females there, reading to me out of the Bible. You can imagine my thoughts: sinful! I didn't know what to make of this religious movement. At one stage, we were all in a circle. Some women were thanking the Lord — they'd had hardships — and they were thanking the Lord for the help he sent them; they knelt down. You'll probably never believe it, but it's the honest truth. I'll take the oath for all I'm going to tell you; I won't exaggerate anything. One woman thanked the Lord for a new electric stove! Others asked the Lord for things they wanted, to keep them going. At the time I wanted a new boat. I didn't ask the Lord publicly, in front of the others, but I asked the Lord if He'd send me a new boat. And the singing! We had hymns. We prayed for my eyesight, 'cos I'd been there two weeks. And it came to Easter time. On the way there the preacher said: "Ed, what's your favourite hymn?" Well, my favourite's 'Onward Christian Soldiers, Marching as to War,' that's my favourite. "All right," he says. We arrived there at the place. There are millions of people who don't know this, but those of you who've read the Bible will know about it: you've read of talking in tongues. Well, different people were mumbo-jumboing there, all sorts of old stuff, and the lady that was really the boss of it, the No. 1 Boss, translated what the Lord had said to us. Well, I'll confess, I didn't really believe too much of it.

But nevertheless, I was there. They started to play the hymns. They had 'Onward Christian Soldiers' and I sang a bit, then another hymn, then 'Onward Christian Soldiers' again. It was just as if I'd had those three pints of ale. You know that would make me drunk. Well, two rounds of 'Christian Soldiers' and a little bit of preaching, I was beginning to get drunk in a different sort of way. I know I sang at the top of my voice and even shouted "Alleluiah", like the others did, after it was all over. I really got emotionally wound up by it. I'm going to tell you a bit more and it's true; at this table everybody had a glass of wine, but I didn't have one and I was pretty thirsty after all this singing. I said to the preacher: "Can I have a drink?" "No," he says: "you ain't a Christian." Well, I felt a bit left out, I can tell you. We had more singing and I sang hard. The No. 1 Boss, this lady preacher woman, started to preach. It must have been almost midnight I should think. The atmosphere was set perfect for it. She said: "Hark! Listen Everybody!" We all listened, and I believed in my mind that the Lord was there and all his Disciples; we were like disciples ourselves. I felt I could have been Matthew, Mark, Luke or John, any of them, it didn't matter. She said: "Waggon's drawing up right here and it's loaded with Christians. We're all on it." It was going to Heaven. "But," she said: "there's room for one more. Miss this chance and you'll never get another one!" Well, I'd missed out on the wine; I wasn't going to miss the last chance to join the Lord. I said: "Stop, I'm coming! I'm going to give myself to the Lord!" Everybody was so thrilled to think I'd given myself to the Lord. "Alleluia, Praise the Lord!" they shouted. I said the same. It was a tremendous experience.

I decided I'd give up swearing, as I say all the naughty words. I'd give up smoking; I wouldn't do the pools or any gambling. Or this is what they wanted me to do. And I said I would do it; I'd really give myself to the Lord, there were no two ways about it: I was a changed man!

I remember, I came home that night. Marie and my parents were watching television. I never said a word to them. I was only thinking of the Lord. A day or two passed, and Mother and Marie got worried. I *wouldna'* swearing, I *wouldna'* my old self. I was always saying to myself, if I was alone, "Praise the Lord". I had religious mania, but I didn't know it at that time. I didn't swear in front of anybody and all I talked of was the Lord, all the time in our house; and I always was trying to convert more Christians. But I know, one night I came to bed; Marie was already in. I got into my pyjamas and walked to my side. We had one of those fancy things on top of the bed with tassels round the bottom. I didn't know it, but our cat Tom was underneath the bed. As I got near the bed I must have put my toes underneath the tassels. The cat reached right down and scratched and bit my foot. I tell you right now, I said the most wicked words a man could ever say. Marie laughed and laughed and laughed. She said: "I knew it wouldn't last long." I said: "I'll kill the bastard if I can catch 'in." Then I said: "That's Satan, that's what it is." (I soon had an answer for it). "That's Satan trying to take me away from the Lord."

I was in a trance, day after day, and it really did worry my family. There was to be no more turning back, I can tell you.

But I had an old buddy that came home from working on the motorways, and came specially to see me. I was out at the time. My parents told him: "Kevin," they said: "He's a changed man. He's gone religious. He's got religious mania. He's a different bloke than any of you ever knew." He said: "I'm waiting to see this man." Well, he waited. When we met I thought 'I'll try to take Kevin to one of our meetings.'

He said: "Are you coming down for a drink to the pub?" "No," I says: "I couldn't do that. The Lord wouldn't let me." He carried on. He was determined to get me to the pub. He said: "If the Lord is so strong, he'll give you the strength and you can come to the pub and watch." 'Well,' I thought, 'yes, it would be a good way of demonstrating'. I went to the pub. Somehow or other I had a pint of cider, and another pint, and maybe there was whisky in it as well, I don't know. We started to sing. It was like old times. They talked of the earth moving, the diggers; I was away. They convinced me, the others, it wasn't the life for me. I'd just got to be myself, the way I'd been.

I came back that dinner time, or after the pub closed, and on the way home who should we bump into? The preacher! I was singing and shouting. He said: "Who is your Saviour?" Kevin, my friend, who we'd been on the cider with, replied: "St Austell Brewery is our saviour." The poor old preacher nearly dropped dead. He said: "Praise the Lord!" Kevin said: "Praise the Lord too; we'm here and we'm happy." Well, I can tell you, back at the religious headquarters they were pretty upset. Marie said: "If you ever go back again, I'll leave you for it. I'll have no part of that." I rang the No. 1 Boss up (she was coming to see me, they wouldn't let me go), I said: "If you come to my house, my family will be very rude." She said: "What are they saying?" This was maybe a couple of hours after I'd come back from the pub; I was still under the influence of drink. I said: "They reckon that you lot's mad and if I carried on I would be mad." "No," she said: "they always say that." But I told her I wouldn't be coming back.

My old granfer, who was nearly eighty, was staying here and after I'd dropped the 'phone there only happened to be Granfer and myself in the front sitting room. I asked Granfer his opinion about it. He said: "Well, boy, have you ever seen a vicar behaving like you was behaving?" "No," I says. He said: "Have you ever seen a chapel minister behave like that?" "No," I says. He says: "Have you ever seen a Catholic priest behave like that?" "No," I says: "never." "No," he said: "because they got more bloody sense than you've got." And that is about it. I had experienced religious mania.

I want to say really how I feel about religion. You'll say to yourselves: 'Well, Ed, with no education, you aren't too clever, you were easy prey for them!' Well, I can tell you something: the majority of them that were religious maniacs were more clever than most people; they could talk four or five languages, they could add up sums or do anything. They were super brains, they were *'lite*. No, I was the odd one out. If it happened to me, it could happen to anybody: no need to have brains, or you can have brains, to be caught with religious mania. Falling in love with the Lord is like falling in love with a woman too quickly. I was already attached to the Lord, I believed in Him. I didn't need them to get hold of me. It was something that was already there; I loved Him. I went silly with myself and this is what happens to religious maniacs. There's thousands of them, millions I bet, throughout the world. You've just got to be yourself; I think the Lord wouldn't want me to be that way, or anybody else. He just wants you to be yourself and make people happy, and do as much good in the world as you can to other people. He doesn't want you going around and shouting 'Alleluia' at the top of your voice and making a damn fool of yourself; He wants you to get out in the field, just ordinary people, and do your best. That's basically how I feel.

CHAPTER 14

Faith Healing

WELL, I'D GOT OVER all that lot. What an experience, eh? Easter had gone and I soon started to paint the boat up and get ready; go to Padstow May Day, for the 'Obby 'Oss, and then the visitors start to come and the fishing. I know, I used to go lots to Padstow or Trevose Lifeboat Station, where the Padstow lifeboat's kept. There I was to get very friendly with the coxswain, called Gordon Elliott. Gordon had two sons. I can always remember them because they had names from the Bible: Simon and Luke. I know, one day I went there and Gordon gave me the biggest surprise I had in my life, something that I'll always remember. He said: "Ed, if you're up tomorrow morning you can have a day with me on the lifeboat. It's Lifeboat Day at Port Isaac. I'd like you to come with me."

I really didn't sleep that night. I arrived there. Gordon blew the whistle, Pat Rabey hit the pin, and we hurtled down that there slipway like tram running down a tunnel in a tin mine. We hit the water and away we went. We were in the lifeboat in raging seas, just out past Merope Rocks. It was just like a February night. I was up in the bridge with Gordon. What a skipper!

Gordon then paid me the highest compliment he could: he actually asked me for a trip out in my little boat. I couldn't believe it. It would be something like Brian Clough (well, you all know who he is, the football manager) asking to come and manage your own local football team, that's what the feeling would be like. Gordon came down with his two sons. Yes, we used to go to sea together, Gordon steering my little boat with the outboard engine, two-and-a-half miles out to sea, to a place called the Gulland Rock, young Simon and Luke with us, fishing. Gordon used to keep this dinghy close to the big rock out there and I know on a couple of occasions there was a fair bit of swell. I never doubted Gordon's ability as a boat handler; we

could have stepped ashore anytime and climbed onto the Rock.
But there, that was Gordon, he didn't need a compass to get
home in a fog. He told me and taught me a lot about the sea. He
was a fantastic guy. I'll never forget 'un as long as I live. Neither
will the people nor the crew of the Padstow lifeboat. He was a
great man, but poor old Gordon had to retire from the Padstow
lifeboat through ill-health. When the rockets went and he
couldn't go on the lifeboat, it almost killed him. So his wife had
to take him away from the Padstow area in the end, and soon he
died.

They were real special days down on that lovely little sandy
beach, down at On-John's Cove with the holiday people; and
when I had the coxswain of Padstow lifeboat to take me to sea,
that was great. I must have been the luckiest bloke in all the
world. Well, I think so anyhow.

I know from then onwards as I told you, I used to go regularly
to spiritual meetings, because I used to get such terrible pains in
my left eye, where I'd run the steel in, but there was a healer at
St Austell that really did help it. I felt much better after I came
home, and it would last for quite a long time. But sometimes
there would be mediums there so I had things told me and I got
mixed up quite a lot with spiritualism. As I'd got caught with
religious mania I planned no one was ever going to sell me
anything more to do with religious mania, unless I thought they
were genuine. I never did see anybody with religious mania at
the spiritual meeting. They came from all denominations. They
were just ordinary people. Some perhaps didn't lead as good
lives as they should. They talked about supernatural powers
and reincarnation and told some fantastic stories. It was just up
my street. I enjoyed every minute of it. I know, once I was there
a medium told me that I had healing powers. I could help
people. You don't need to be a spiritualist to have spiritual
healing powers; you've no need to belong to any religious
movement whatsoever. Millions of people have got it and never
use it. You've no need to put your hands on someone, but it's
like the Royal Touch; from a special healer, you feel better if
they do touch you. Some healers can work and do you a lot of
good that you never know anything about. The situation varies
between healer and the person involved. When they invited me

to give people that were sick healing, I didn't like the idea of it, as I was crocked up myself. I thought it wasn't a good advert for me to be crocked up and helping others.

I always knew if I could help someone. I'd no need to touch them. I'm not kinky or anything when I say that if they were in trouble, I could help them spiritually; there's no two ways about it. There were lots of people with trouble of all sorts: backs, legs, everything.

I know there was one old lady who couldn't come. So we went to see her, this other healer and myself (the other healer was a female). I know, we had a hard job to get in: Jane's poodle was almost mad, but he did let us in in the end. Jane had lost her husband about two months before we got there. She said she felt terrible, she had rheumatism and mentally she was down. I just talked to her, not like a preacher. Jane was maybe sixty-five or even more; I called her Jane, she told me to, although she was a lady. I said: "Jane, when things go wrong in life and you lose a partner, it's like losing a man overboard on a ship; if you give up you never make it back to port; you've got to forget that and sail on and bring the ship home. That's like your body, that's the ship; you've got to keep on sailing to bring it home." I think we cheered her up. We did put our hands, lay our hands, upon this woman. We made several visits. I know almost six months, or maybe even twelve months later, I rang up the healer at Padstow and I said: "How's Jane?" "She don't need the money, but she's got a little job now at Lanhydrock* as a guide, showing people around." I said: "She's really better?" "Yes," she said: "and she always claims that you and I cured her."

In 1978 Jane left the County of Cornwall and the healer from Padstow told me soon after that Jane had passed away, but she did have some years, some happy years, here in Cornwall.

But there, that's it, that's life. We can't stay here for ever. It would be nice in this world if everyone could get cured and just die of old age. But there, we all know it can't be that way exactly.

The next situation I was going to run across was with a friend I've got, a farmer. I know I was over at his farm one day, and I was walking around and I saw his dog lying on two bales of straw. I said: "What's up here, Captain?" "Oh, Ed," he said:

*A house belonging to the National Trust

"dog's been bad for weeks and weeks, and yet he was a good worker, sheep and everything. It seems terrible to see him lying out on the bales of straw." He said: "I've took 'in to the veterinary there's nothing they can do. I haven't got the heart to have him put down; when's good weather I put 'in out, Ed, when it's rough I take 'un in." The farmer loved his dog more than all his acres; you couldn't put a price on that dog. I said: "Look, I know a friend that's a faith healer, I'll tell him about your dog." I didn't like to say it was me. But I went very close to the dog and just layed my hands on him, rubbed his legs and his face; he lay there so helpless. I did ask the Lord if He'd make this dog better. I said: 'It would please me and the farmer. It would make so much happiness if this dog would run and do the things he wants to once more, chase the sheep and maybe the odd cat that's in and out; and live a good life.' I know I went for a few weeks and I used to look in on the dog. But I never did forget him; I thought about him for a long, long time. It was almost twelve months before I went back that way again. I was in the little, narrow road. I heard a movement. I had the beautifullest surprise: this lovely black and white collie dog sprang off the hedge, just like a kangaroo, and landed right down by my feet and came right for' by my side. I said: "Captain: the dog's better." "Oh yes!" he said: "He's been better for a long, long time." He said: "It was nothing short of a real miracle." He said: "I went down to the house one morning, to bring him out and before I got down there I heard him squealing and shouting; he was up on his legs and wanted to get running around." Well, the Lord did answer my prayers and that dog is still alive today.

I found, being a faith healer you get a lot of good things happen to you and a lot of bad things, but I don't want to depress you with any of the failures.

CHAPTER 15

Christopher Starts Work

MY NEXT APPOINTMENT was going to be at Moorfields again. They wanted to see what the retina was like on my left eye, that I ran the piece of steel in. They also wanted to get this bit of steel out. So Marie and I set sail for Moorfields once more.

I decided this time I wasn't going to have any trouble with the nurses. I was going to butter 'em up a bit. I was going to use all the old charm a man can ever use on 'em. Wasn't going to cheek 'em or make things awkward. Well: it worked! They spoiled me, and treated me like a baby. They did sure enough. I got very friendly with the other patients that were in. I met a vicar there from Jersey and other, different people; all nationalities I met. I suppose I stole the stage. I talked about smuggling days and wrecking and things that we do down here in Cornwall; about curses and superstitions and all the lot. The vicar enjoyed it as much as the rest of them. That was good, but the operation side of things wasn't.

The surgeon told me that he could see the little hole where the piece of steel had gone in a long way. He said: "Ed, it's like a woodworm gone into a piece of wood. You can see the hole but you can't see the bit, the damaging bit. We couldn't go any farther," he said. Doctors are like politicians, when they don't want you to understand something, they talk in big words. When they want you to understand something, they talk in easy language, like I use. This doctor went on to say: "Ed," he says: "your eye is like a television camera. If I fired a rifle bullet through that television camera, it would be ruined, it would never work again, and that's just like what's happened to your eye." I knew exactly what he meant.

Poor old Marie was really disappointed. But there, the operation all done, I had a day or two to get over it, and then we went down to Paddington Station. I had dark glasses on. Oh my God!

My eyes were so sore it was terrible! I caught hold of Marie's arm and we walked around Paddington Station. I kept my eyes closed; it was the only way I could get peace. I kept saying: "Make sure nobody don't run into us, Marie." I could hear all those little trucks chuttering away, and people going. "No, you're all right," she said. Marie was a nurse in a Mental Nursing Hospital. She knew how to look after a patient. I was her special patient. What a woman Marie was to look after me like that.

But there; home we came once more to Cornwall. By this time Christopher had left school and got a job. Now you're wondering where'd he work? Well, I'll tell you, he worked for Mid-Cornwall Contractors. I suppose Christopher got in at the back door, as I knew everybody, and, for good measure, he learned his apprenticeship with my best friend, Douggie Duguid. Before he went there to work, I rang Douggie Duguid one night to say I didn't want any special favours for my son. I said: "It will be no achievement for you, if he turns out a failure. I want you to turn out somebody good, Doug. Be strict. Teach him the hard way." Apprentices, in the olden days, were dipped in a trough and there were certain rituals. I know that's all gone now and it was all gone in Christopher's day. It was my wish that Doug would be hard and rule Chris with a rod of iron. It's the way I like it. And as sure as God made little apples that's what Douggie Duguid did do. If Christopher did anything wrong, he had ways of punishing him. I suppose you can call it weakeners, giving him the rough jobs. If he did well, he'd be rewarded, and things were going happily at that end.

I know I told you, Marie was good at giving me surprises. The next surprise she gave me was a metal detector, because I was on the beach one day and I borrowed someone else's and I found an old half-a-crown and a brooch within a few seconds. You didn't need eyes, you could be totally blind to work a metal detector! But Marie gave me a beautiful one. It was really good. I found many coins, almost bucket loads of 'em. I found lots of rings, some of 'em I've still got here, in this house now. But the thing I discovered when I was prospecting was: people would always come and talk to me and ask me about treasures. And almost one out of five, if they were ladies, would say: "Well, would it find a wedding ring?" And I'd say: "Yes, of course it would, why?" And then they used to tell me stories of how they'd lost their wedding ring or their engagement rings or friends had, and soon a lady in the village asked me if I could find a ring that one of her boy friends had lost. I did find that particular one, and I went on and I found many, many rings for people. I realised that people are more superstitious over rings they wear on their fingers than anything else. I learned this from talking to many people.

So you know basically how my life is set now. In the summer fishing, with people taking me out in my boat and perhaps finding rings for visitors in the evening, if they lose them. And, in the winter, prospecting, wrecking, if there is any wood around, and if Marie was going shopping to any little village or town in Cornwall, I used to love to go. It was really good to have a day off with Marie.

CHAPTER 16

Living It Up!

BUT I KNOW in that year, of '73, we fell out a fair bit. We had many a row. The old saying 'Wives and waves don't mix', well, 'tis true really. Marie said to me one night: "I feel like going down and smash that boat up or paying someone to do it." She said: "I just can't stop you. I can't keep you away from that boat. It's just like another woman that's come between us, Ed. Sometimes I wish it was. I would know how to handle it then. But I don't know how to stop you from that boat." No, I don't suppose Marie did know how to stop me, because it's in my blood; my ancestors were fishermen from Port Isaac, going back hundred years; so it's still there.

But there it is: instead of going to work and coming home at five, tired, to wash and sit down and watch the television, I was a changed person: I was leading a different sort of life, 'cos on the beach I was meeting the *'lite*. I suppose that's the right word. Well, put it this way: I met everybody from doctors, bank managers, managers of big companies, to people in finance; I met everybody at the top. I met people from Henley, I've got many friends there; many friends all over Great Britain. If I'd been on the water maybe four or five hours with some of these people they'd very often invite me and maybe Marie out for a drink, or a barbecue on the beach or something. Marie nearly always declined to come. Sometimes I went to these parties against Marie's will and things weren't really how they should be back at this house. Old Marie was always glad when summer was over and everybody had gone. She would take over then and I would be hers. I know that year, Marie gave me the greatest surprise ever. She bought me a coloured television set, a real great big one. She worked and saved her money and bought that as a special present for me. When I came home, there it was, going for me. In fact I was so pleased with it I never went out for about two days or three days. I even just watched the picture card that was up there and the colours were fantastic. It was great. I stand up close and get the idea of what a programme looks like: the speakers' faces, a play's dress and the characters; then I sit back and imagine from what is just a blur.

But there we are: Marie was never to give up on my eye-sight. Unbeknown to me she'd planned a trip to Italy. She'd read, in the papers, of some famous eye surgeon. She'd got her brother to make arrangements at that end. It was something special when we went down to see the doctor. I think 'twas down near Naples. We were four of us in the car, plus the driver. Everybody came into the hospital and all into the doctor's surgery. But there it is: he looked into my eyes and he told Marie it was impossible. Poor old Marie: it was hard for me to see her upset about it, when I really knew (and Granny Taylor told me) there wasn't much hope for that eye that was damaged. I knew it myself, but there we are: there was always a chance I could have been wrong and Marie could have been right. But it was no good. It was a wasted journey, but we had a happy holiday there and then we came back home.

The next thing that was going to happen to me was something special. I'd bought myself a dog. I'm going to tell you that at the end of the story, that'll be the last bit. To cheer you up! But you'll just have to wait for it!

Life went on. Christmas went by and we were into the New year of '74. I said at the beginning of my story you only remember the good things and the bad. You'll know why I remember '74 when I tell you the next episode in my life.

Summer came along. I'd got the boat painted and ready for another season. But I want you to place your minds back a little bit. You remember how I told you I saw that gipsy girl, the fortune teller at Royal Cornwall Show, when she told me I'd meet another woman? Well, another woman did come into my life. I never planned for it, it just happened, through the boat and on Harlyn Beach and On-John's Cove.

Now I think I'd better put one thing straight to you right away: I don't plan on talking about this too much.

I met this woman on On-John'sCove. She was like a red, rustic sunset. Well, you all know how beautiful that looks and you also know it brings forth something good the next day. I'm not joking, everybody passed remarks about her on the beach. She could charm a swarm of bees out of the beehive on a frosty day. She had the personality. She could talk to any person, it didn't matter if they were rich or poor. She was a fantastic woman.

As the days rolled by this woman fell in love with me. You can always tell when somebody has flipped their lid. If it's religion, fallin' in love with a man or a woman, or when you get obsessed by something, you can always tell. I knew she had it bad for me. Soon I was going to fall in love with this other woman. I felt a bit wicked as she had a husband, but I knew she was only there for another four months, she wasn't a local woman, she'd be leaving this area. To make myself feel easier I thought: 'Well, who would miss a grain of sand off Harlyn Beach? Nobody wouldn't!' So I carried on with this woman.

We fooled most people, we really did. Nobody could believe it, that a smart young woman would ever get mixed up with someone that's partially blind and didn't work. I never had a reputation, I could be trusted; an Arab Sheik would almost trust me with his harem. I never told Marie. She never asked. They used to say in the old days 'the darkest place is by the hurricane lamp'. 'Well,' I thought 'that's the way I'll play it: wide open.'

But it came up to the end of summer and I hadn't been caught. I was really in love. I had two women. I had Marie. I had this other woman. I didn't know what to do. If somebody said: 'Ed, you've got to leave Great Britain, you're only allowed to take two women', I should have taken Marie and this woman. There was no doubt about it, I didn't hate Marie. I had two super women, but a man in this country can't be married to two women.

This woman wanted me to leave Marie and come with her. I told her: "I couldn't do it, not here, not in Cornwall. The people of our village would never stand for it." They really would never have stood for it. I couldn't do that. I said: "If I come with you, we've got to leave Cornwall; that's it, never come back no more."

We didn't discuss that too much, anyhow. It came time that she would soon be going, leaving with her husband. We made arrangements that we wouldn't lose contact. She'd telephone me or get in contact with me some way or other. But we had a farewell party, as usual. We always do down here, when all the children and the people here on holiday at the end of August go back: a last farewell till another year. I didn't want to go, but this woman insisted. I wanted Marie to go, but she wouldn't. This other woman's husband was there too, but I danced with this woman. I had a few dances with one of the others; the husband danced with a few. This woman, I kept on dancing with her. Half-way through, an atmosphere rang through the room. I had the feeling that there was trouble, as much as if somebody had been murdered outside. You get the feeling when things aren't right. I was dancing with this woman and she told me the bad news: "Ed," she said: "my husband knows everything." I said: "Who's told him?" She said: "Another holiday-maker from On-John's Cove. Another woman." And, for good measure, she was a school teacher.

This woman was here for another fortnight. I know Marie and I were rowing terrible. Marie's never told me, but I'm sure she knew all about it; she was no fool. She told me she was going home. You'll hate me for this, what I'm going to tell you now, but it's no good telling lies. She wanted to go home, and needed some money. I said: "Right, drive me to St Columb bank and I'll draw out some money and you can go home." Whoever could do this to a woman who had taken him all around Europe just about, and Great Britain and done good for him all her life? And I did this to her! We went to St Columb. Marie cried her eyes out. I wasn't calling her bluff this time. I really meant it. But she couldn't go through with it, and we drove back home. She asked me, coming back over Winnard's Perch, as you get to the top of the *nip,* "Ed, what is the matter?" I said: "Nothing; just give me time and things will come right."

But soon this woman was going to pack her bags and go. She told me before she left that she was definitely getting a divorce. Her marriage was finished. She said: "Ed, it's over," but I'd never met her in a romantic way since the dance: that was it, she was leaving.

But there: like the old saying 'Time's a great healer'.. And it did come better as the months rolled by.

I know Marie made an appointment for me to go to a fortune-teller with her. We drove to Plymouth. I went in first and saw this woman. She seemed to soon get on the track, how I'd had a mistress and other things. She didn't give me too much advice. She just told me that I'd see this woman again; soon, but only once more. Marie saw this fortune-teller as well. A month later we went back again. And I'll say to all of you, 'cos I know a lot of you ladies do go to fortune-tellers and you never tell anybody about it and you never tell the truth what these fortune-tellers tell you, but I got told this: that I was to give Marie nothing but the best and I wasn't to upset her whatsoever because in three-and-a-half years something was going to happen to her; she was going to die.

I knew that I had to look after Marie, I also knew that this woman and her husband had completely broken up. I used to telephone her at her work. She didn't force me to come with her. She said: "If Marie goes, if you break up, I want you to come with me." That's what she said. I thought of the fortune-teller, what she told me about the three-and-a-half years. I thought: 'Well she might just be right, so if I do go and Marie dies, I'll have that on my conscience until the end of my days.' I also took into consideration my love for Cornwall, for On-John's Cove and Harlyn Bay. I knew if I went I'd never be able to come back. I'd have to live in exile for the rest of my life.

And so, as time went on I began to love Marie once more. It was something like the experience with religious mania. Once that had passed, given time, things came right once more. And for the next two years I gave Marie love and loyalty (I know they both begin with l), but loyalty to me is a bit more special than love is.

How can I describe the difference between love and not-love? The difference is like a flower that's a beautiful flower that smells and a beautiful flower that doesn't. That's how I describe it. I suppose there was one person that was well qualified to answer that question. That was the king of England who went to live with Mrs Simpson. He gave up the throne of England

and he lived in exile. He had more courage than I ever had. I just couldn't do it.

After about twelve months had passed, I telephoned this woman and she told me she had another boy friend. It was no more than I expected, because I predicted to her one day on On-John's Cove what would happen. I told her she'd meet someone. I said: "You'll really hate me." She wouldn't believe it. She said: "No, never." I said: "You really will." But now she told me she'd got a boy friend, she would soon be divorced and marry this other man. I thought no more about it. But one day, in our village of St Merryn, I bumped into this woman. I can tell you straight it was one of the biggest shocks I ever had in my life, 'cos I never thought she'd come back here again.

But there she was with a new husband. To me, the feeling at that time was like being swept off the rocks, by a giant freak wave. It caught me out of the blue. As she spoke, I said: "I don't know who you are." She said: "You must do." And then I realised it. I couldn't speak for a second or two, but as she knew all about me she carried on the conversation and then I gathered myself together. I didn't talk to her and her husband very much. They'd come down here for their honeymoon on the South Coast, not on the North Coast. But, she said: "I wanted to see On-John's Cove once more, Ed." I just had a few seconds to talk to her on her own. I just wished her well and all the happiness in the world.

So the fortune-teller was right, I did only see her that one more time.

CHAPTER 17

Cockle-Riding

IN A VILLAGE, people don't like it when a man does what I did. Marie was so good and worked so hard and gave me everything, and I did that behind her back. They didn't like it.

In the olden days they used to call it cockle-riding. You might laugh when I say that, but it's serious stuff, I can tell you. They gave this the name, because on Padstow Doom Bar you could go out and get as many cockles as you wanted to, it was easy, but you paid a price, 'cos it was dangerous to get these cockles; you all know what a doom bar's like, doesn't matter if it's in the Padstow Estuary or anywhere else in the world, many a ship's been wrecked there and many lives lost. The sea can come in around you and gobble you up like a giant, man-eating shark; the fog can set down quick and you get lost. And that's why they called it in Cornwall cockle-riding.

And, in the olden days, for cockle-riding, if you were caught and found out, if you were married, the vicar would organise what they called a shaming party. He'd get all the old pots and pans, metal ones, and from the blacksmith's shop any old bits of iron and they'd go to the women's house first and maybe tar or whitewash her house. And then they'd go on to the man's place and do the same, banging the metal outside. And then go to the beach, wherever it might be, at Rock, Padstow or anywhere, and there they'd burn an effigy of the two people; and that used to stop 'em. That old tradition has died out around here. That's over and done with. But the thing is, they still don't like cockle-riding, not when you're married. You might think to yourself 'Well how could they punish you?' They've got ways and means of doing it. We're one big family down here: they turn your taps off; by that I mean your privileges, no one will do you any favours any more. You'd be locked out. That's partly why I had to stay home here in St Merryn. But they didn't hold it against me, 'cos I was loyal. I never ran away from Marie; that was what mattered most.

Marie and I had settled down pretty fair. Chris was about eighteen. He hadn't fully served his apprenticeship as heavy duty plant fitter, but one day he was home from work, looking through the paper and he saw a job advertised in Dubai, that's in the State of Oman. He said: "Father, I'm going to apply for that job." Well, instantly I thought: 'A boy that hasn't qualified will stand no chance.' His mother nearly had a heart attack when he said he was going. So did his gran and granfer. But when Christopher went out I convinced them that it was impossible that he'd ever get the job. I said: "They want qualified men about twenty-three to twenty-five, not young boys that don't know much." Well, they all agreed with me. I said: "Just let him go and he'll get turned down and it'll be out of his system and he'll never mention it no more. We fight him, he'll never be contented nowhere."

Well, he wrote about this job. Soon, he had word to go for an interview at London. He rang me from London, and I just about had a heart attack. He says: "Father, I have got the job!" I said: "When do you go?" He said: "In two weeks' time." God Almighty! It was really hell in this house. Marie and my father and mother played hell with me. They said it was all my fault, I encouraged it. I encouraged it 'cos it was in my mind that on the technical side of things it was impossible; but on the spiritual side of things it wasn't impossible. But there he was; Christopher was soon to leave his good job, without having served his apprenticeship, and go to Dubai.

Before he'd been there a fortnight he was a bit homesick. He was working with about five or six hundred men of all nationalities. But he was lucky; he met a man then called Fred Lees who had lost his son in a motor-bike accident. The boy was Christopher's age when he got killed, and this chap took Christopher under his wing; and he stayed there until the end of the contract.

Then he came home and worked in Scotland. The Dubai Company sent him a telegram one day, asking if he'd like to come back again; they had more work. I was really worried this time. I knew something would happen. Honest to God, I did. I thought he'd be jacking up a dumper and it would fall on him.

But I couldn't stop him from going, it had to happen.

I know a week or two previously I'd found an old silver two shilling piece on the beach, and I gave it to Chris for good luck. I said: "Don't lose it, don't spend it; that's going to bring you home safe, Chris."

When we were at Paddington Station, we had a cup-of-tea: Christopher, his mama, me and his girl-friend. Christopher bought the tea and before he left us at Paddington I said: "Have you still got the two shillings?" "No," he said: "I spent it getting the tea." As I'm superstitious, I knew then there'd be trouble. I never told Marie or anyone. I was really worried. But he was gone. He sent us a telegram to say he'd arrived all right.

A fortnight passed. I'd come home from the beach and found Marie was in a terrible way. She said: "Something's happened to Christopher. He's in hospital. The man's going to 'phone back here at six o'clock to talk to you." The man rang, and told me that Christopher was out working on a job late at night and another fitter was driving and the Landrover capsized, or turned over right upside down, and Chris had broken the vertebrae, or something in his neck. He was alive and they'd get him home as soon as he was well enough to travel. God Almighty! There it was. Soon Christopher was home.

Well, he got better a little bit and went to work once more, back at St Austell. He only worked a week and then he was taken terribly ill again with his back and neck. Back in plaster, he was like an old chicken that was hatching from an egg; you know when they look out of the top of the egg; the plaster was right up his back and up to his chin. The doctor told me: "Your son'll never work again. No heavy work, I'm sorry to say this, but he'll have to have a little, light job in an office." I thought: 'Well, I never! That's two of us on the scrap heap!' So I did Marie's job; I took Christopher on the long trail to different healers that I knew. We went to places where they almost had religious mania. I told Christopher: "Don't get caught by it, you're only coming for the healing." He was strong by my side. The others used to fall on the floor, and go berserk, but we were all right; we were the only two who would walk in and walk out, just like we are now.

All that summer, Christopher spent his time on On-John's Cove, in the boat house, sitting on a fish box, looking out to sea. He'd see me off with visitors and see me come back. All my friends from Great Britain used to join him in the boat house and talk to him.

I know, a friend told me once I should take him to a man called Mr Richards. He'd not got a reputation as a faith healer, but he'd helped many people. I took Christopher there (he drove the car). On the first visit Christopher said: "Father, that man is just magic. I can feel the heat going right through my body. I must come back again." We did go back again for about eight more visits. When he came out of the plaster, the doctor was thrilled.

Christopher started to work at home around here on farms, chucking round bales of straw, and he got fit. But he also had a little stroke of luck: his boss, one of the Arab men he knew in Oman, started a new company. His foreman was home in the UK and came to see Christopher. He told him how he was going back to work for this Arab: "Any chance of a job, Chris, I'll try and get you out!" Within a fortnight the 'phone went. This was Mohammed Backer. He wanted Chris to come out. Christopher said: "I don't know if I'll pass the medical." "Who's worried about a medical?" He said: "I want you to come out." Well, Christopher was gone in three days. In 1979 he was only twenty-three and he'd climbed right to the top of the tree for his age. He was workshop foreman. These Arabs think the world of my son, but my son is just like me: somebody has given him a chance (he most probably would never have got a job at home); that Arab had given my son a chance and he doesn't want to let him down. He works from seven in the morning to half-past seven at night. Maybe he only has one day off in three months. He gives his boss the best; he's happy, just like I was at work. Things came perfect for Chris.

CHAPTER 18

The Break Up

BUT THERE WAS ONE more thing to happen to me. Things were pretty good with me and Marie but she had a lady's complaint and had to have an operation called a hysterectomy. She decided to go to stay with another nurse, who had lost her husband and had a few acres of land near St Austell. She decided to go there when she came out of hospital for a week or two. She did do this, and then came home for a little bit. She started to go there more and more, for three weeks at a time; four weeks. Then, when she came home to see my mother, she'd cook and clean and do all Mother's work, work like a slave. Then she'd go away and maybe she'd have taken a dress out of the wardrobe. Her wardrobe was getting less and less. She had put all my pullovers right, all my clothes with little mini safety-pins so I'd know which was front and back. She organised everything for me right to the end. Then, one day, she asked me for a divorce, which I granted. I said she could. That's what I said to you: that's the difference between love, a flower that smells and a flower that doesn't. I said I would grant the divorce, so from that 5th April '79, we were parted. It was all over. But just for a little bit of good measure, one of the holiday-makers I knew on the beach, whom I was friendly with for more than ten or eleven years, left his wife, and Marie left Cornwall and went to live somewhere else in Great Britain with this friend.

The old fortune-teller was wrong, but I don't regret being nice to Marie for the last three-and-a-half years. I only wished I was nicer. I don't want you to hate the mistress I had. She was under the impression that I was unhappy with Marie: I was under the impression that she was unhappy with her husband. I'm delighted she married that other chap, for her sake. She didn't want to be stuck with somebody like me.

Marie, she's still Number One for me. She's the best in the world. She gave me twenty years — twenty of the greatest years I'll have in my life. She did me no harm. I wish her well too. I don't suppose for one minute she'll ever come back to our village with that chap. She lived long enough in Cornwall to know Cornish ways and Cornish people: she'd get the feeling.

Now I don't want you to feel sorry for me, or anything like that, 'cos I deserved every bit that came my way. If you want to do any good for me, don't feel sorry. Just wish me luck. Wishing people luck will do a lot of good. You'll never imagine what good that'll do for a person. That's what I want you to do for me. But I'm happy enough, I really am. I had my dog, that I'll be telling you about, and my little bit of ground.

I didn't tell you, an old fortune-teller told me I would build a house. By nothing short of a miracle — but that's another story — I got planning permission for a little plot of ground away out in the country, on its own, with lovely green fields and birds and foxes around me, and slowly with my compensation money I'm building that up. It's important for me to tell you just how I got that piece of ground. When I lived at Trewithen this little bit of ground lay idle, and when I was a young lad (I mean about seven or eight) I used to *teal* my crops in this piece of land that was walled-in to build a house there. The man that owned it decided to go to Padstow to live. But when I grew up to the age of about seventeen, he stopped one night and he saw how hard I worked on this little piece of land, with all my crops. He gave me a lot of praise. He said: "Edward, I think you ought to pay me maybe sixpence a year rent, but I'd rather for you to buy it off me." I said: "How much do you want for it?" He said: "I want one hundred pounds." I said: "Well, I don't know." Because I didn't have a hundred pounds. He said: "Well, anyhow, just come along and see me one night." Which I did. I went to see this man, called Mr Hawkins. He's passed away now. But at the time I told him the truth. I said: "I'm not being cheeky in what I'm going to say: all's I've got to my name is fifty pounds." He looked at me. He said: "Edward, I want you to have that piece of land — and don't never sell it to anyone unless you're forced to. I always wanted you to have that land." And the deal was done and that's how I got the land at Tresallyn Cross. If you look on

your maps of Cornwall you'll see marked Shop, St Merryn — go
due east for one mile, that's where Tresallyn Cross is.

When I was in the construction business I let it slip a little bit
and it started to grow with brambles, but I always used to look
in, I always knew I had the piece of land there. I tried for
planning permission once, but the Council turned me down,
and then I lost my eye-sight; that was the end of it. I went there
a lot then to work in the garden once more, just like I did when I
was a young child; I couldn't see so well, now, but I really
cleaned the place up. I got all the brambles out and the first year
I was home I *tealed* it all 'tirely with potatoes. I got a few of my
work-mates to come along and help me, and I got the whole
place good. I put in for planning permission again and that
miracle happened, but it came too late for Marie, and I was
stuck with planning permission for a bungalow. I didn't quite
know what to do, but spiritually I was told to go ahead with it
and that's exactly what I did.

In the olden days, if a man was poor and he wanted a house,
his boss would give him a piece of land and all his friends would
come and help him to build the walls and put the roof on in one
day. And they called it 'a house in a day'. That was his, his
property. Well, my house isn't a house in day, but the atmosphere
is just the same. I know I've got some compensation money to
use on the house, but all my friends come, weekends, and give
me little bits to go towards that house and slowly we're completing
it. That piece of land, it just came my way, easily for me, and at
the end of the day it will be finally completed. It was the dream I
always wanted, because I've never really lived on my own,
except once at Plymouth. It was something I always wanted for
Marie, but it came too late.

Tresallyn Cross: it was believed that a saint stopped there,
because it actually has an old cross. My house will be
the same as any house, just three bedrooms and kitchen, a
sitting room and a garage. It isn't the house that is important to
me. The house is important to a woman, that's her place of
work, but to me what is important is what I'm going to do
outside.

You all know of Stonehenge, and that a lot of religious things
took place there. I know a little bit more about stones in

Cornwall. We've got stones put in the ground into a complete circle, that we call Seven Sisters or Nine Maidens. That's where 'the healing' took place; that was where the religious things of long ago happened, and that's why the granite stones were put there to remember that special place. There've been thousands of books written about this, but I don't know what the other people said. This is just my theory and what I've been told. So what do Nine Maidens mean? You all know a number 10: the one is a man and the 'ought is a woman, but Nine Maidens are nine people and they are worshipping Man himself, the Lord, if you want to believe it. So now you've got the feeling of all that, I'll tell you I'm going to have my own Seven Sisters. I'm also having my own rocking stone. Maybe some of you don't know what a rocking stone is: to my knowledge there are two in Cornwall; there's one down West and one somewhere on Bodmin Moor. A rocking stone is for swearing oaths, and used in fertility rites. In the olden days, there were people called white witches; basically they were like a modern-day faith healer. The white witch sometimes used the rocking stone to help people. So I'm going to have one in my pad. So that'll make three then to my knowledge in Cornwall.

You may think: 'Well, Edward, whatever do you want this for?' Well, if you engage a plumber it is no good if he hasn't got any tools to work with, and I'm going to have these tools right at Tresallyn Cross. On each side of the gate I'm having a Celtic cross fitted on one side and a big round ring, cut out of slate on the other side. For the entrance drive, I've spent countless hours in finding different sized stones and different colours (I'm lucky that the Good Lord has left me enough sight to tell the colours between the stones). I'm planning on cobbling all my drive in religious charm rings, so everyone you step in should bring you a bit of luck. 'Cos one day I'm hoping if anybody come to my house, when they leave me they might feel a lot better for it, and then I'll have achieved everything I set out to do. So I'm hoping one day lots of you will be able to come to Tresallyn Cross when I have completed everything.

CHAPTER 19

Reflections

I HOPE YOU HAVE borne with me. I might have contradicted myself. I may have said one thing one day and another thing later on. It's like sewing corn in the field, once it go down the drill rows, that's it. It's a hard job to go round and gather all the grains up and have another go!

Sometimes I've said: "I swear on the Bible that is right." I say that quite a lot, I know. The reason is, we all tell lies. I don't tell lies now, perhaps just one a month. I very much doubt that authors of all the books that are autobiographies could hold a Bible in their hands and swear under oath that they had told the complete truth.

I've found it very difficult and hard to tell you the truth, I'll confess that to you. If I lived in Birmingham, Manchester or Liverpool or any great big, famous city in a high-rise flat and nobody knew me, it would be easier. But here in Cornwall, if I told lies, everybody would know it. If I'd got any skeletons in the cupboard, somebody would soon point it out to me. There's one thing I can swear under oath, I've no skeletons in the cupboard. I've virtually never stolen anything; I've never cheated my bosses out of time or anything; everybody knows that. The ony thing that I ever did very wrong was cockle-riding. But there, that's behind me now. I've got to forget all about it.

I'm home here in Trevithick Estate with just my aged mother and father, both over their seventies. Everything that Marie catered for me lasted about twelve months; all the pins have gone from my pullovers. All my clothes and everything that were packed away in drawers have got shifted around. I haven't got a clue where any documents are. But I remember an old foreman once said to me: "Ed, as long as everybody's moving and working and the job is going on, don't worry about it."

And that's how life is for me: I'm happy enough each day and I'm getting by, so I'm not worried too much about where my Birth Certificate is, or any of the documents; everything seems to be going on all right and that's the way it's got to be for the time.

There may be other stories. My life is like the Celtic Sea itself: it never stays flat, but it'll never be rough for a long time. Winds, waves, and everything are all changing every hour of the day, and that's almost what my life is like. It keeps me excited 'cos I know I've always got something to look forward to.

I've told you my story because I can't read nor write, but to make sure that all the kids can read and write; so they'll be cleverer, and by being cleverer will feed themselves and help the country and the world in general. I also set out to tell you a bit about Cornwall, so most of you people from up country, even those who live here, get to know Cornish people a little bit better.

I feel a bit sad really to be finishing off. Well, if you'm sad, you know you'm soon going to be laughing, so maybe I'll have a super day tomorrow, on the beach, gathering stones.

My Dog Crusader

CRUSADER, that was the name of my Pyrenean Mountain Dog. He was like a stream, running into a water wheel. You may think to yourself: 'I haven't quite got that.' I'll describe what a water wheel is a little bit: it's nearly always set in a valley if there's a river running down, or a stream. There are always lovely flowers and wild life around, birds. The water wheel's spinning round, turning out energy and doing a lot of good. So that's really like Crusader was. I want to try and make you as happy as I can; I don't want to go making you shed a tear or two, and I'm sure that would have been Crusader's wish as well. He was a bundle of joy.

Dogs really are a little bit like humans: they've got family trees, just as we have. We're experts in Cornwall in knowing all ours. Well, I know Crusader's, but I'm not going to take you right through it. Crusader's blood place, Pyrenean Mountains; birth place, St Day, Cornwall. I suppose you could call Crusader a bit of a tinner; he was born in a mining village. But Crusader's mama was called Mercy; she was owned by a lady called Mrs Jory, and Mercy gave birth, about nine years ago, to nine Pyrenean Mountain dogs. Five were healthy and strong and four weren't so strong. Five went down in the shed with their mama and four came indoors that night in a box. Mrs Jory thought they'd all be dead by the morning, but she thought: 'Well, you never know.' In the morning there was one still alive; that was Crusader; he'd just made it.

Mrs Jory didn't know what to do. He was very *pinnicky* and fragile. She decided she'd feed him on a spoon with milk, which she did for several weeks. But, in the meantime, she also had a poodle, called Sheba, and she sold Sheba's puppies and Sheba never had anything to do. She used to see Crusader in his little basket, sucking his dummy (yes, he had a dummy, just like a young babby boy) and I suppose Sheba, with a mothering instinct, thought perhaps she could lend a hand. Crusader was perhaps like a foreigner to Sheba, but she didn't care about that. She wanted to offer her services, and one day she climbed into Babby Crusader's basket and started to wipe his face, clean 'im up a little bit, giving him the motherly touch, I suppose. Soon Crusader was to leave off his dummy. He used to nestle into Sheba, his foster-mother, and they became great friends.

The postman used to say to Mrs Jory: "Argh! that dog isn't worth keeping, I should hit 'un on top of the head." "No," she said: "I'm going to keep that one; he'll be all right, he'll be healthy and strong."

And I suppose this is where I came on the scene. One lunchtime I came home from beach, my father was reading the *Guardian** and he always knew I wanted a Pyrenean Mountain Dog. Marie had tried to get me one, but unsuccessfully. He read the advert that there were six Pyreneans for sale. I rang Mrs Jory right away and told her who I was and how I couldn't see very well. She was reluctant to let me have a dog. She said: "You might trip over one of them." "No," I said: "I wouldn't." I almost went down on my hands and knees and begged her to let me have a dog. I even went so far as to say: "Well, you can ring up anyone in St Merryn and find out if I'm worthy of keeping the dog." And I knew nobody would let me down; they knew I was capable and my family was honest and reliable. In the end, she said: "Yes, I'll keep you a dog." I had to wait until Christopher came home from work. He picked up his girl friend and it was almost eight o'clock before we got to Mrs Jory's.

There was one thing about it, I knew we had the right house. When I knocked on the door, the foundations properly shook with the barking; even Chris looked at me and says: "God Almighty! This is the right house." You couldn't mistake it. We went inside and had a little chat. I thought my dog was down in the shed or outside in a kennel somewhere. There were two big dogs running around the kitchen, a big kitchen, and in the end I couldn't wait any longer. I said: "Where's my dog?" She said: "Just a moment." And she went off up to the top of the kitchen and brought him down. I'll never forget his eyes. He came really

*The *Cornish Guardian*, Edward's local weekly

close to me. His eyes were like Victoria Plums. They were beautiful.

I gingerly put my hand on him; he was a big dog then. He was about the size of a big labrador. I told Mrs Jory that I thought he was a pup. "No," she said: "they're nine months old." Well, that was it. I paid her forty pounds. Mrs Jory said that I must have his feed bowl, so that he wouldn't forget his old home. I knew it would be strange for him to have to leave his old home. It was like going to an orphanage and picking up an orphan child. It seemed sort of sad, when I had to take Crusader away. He had to leave his mama, but all his other brothers and sisters were sold, just Crusader was left, that was all; everybody had had the pick of the bunch. Who was worried? I had my dog, Crusader. I didn't call him that; Mrs Jory did. I couldn't have chosen a better name myself.

So we got Crusader into the car, or Mrs Jory did, and we started to head home to North Cornwall Coast and Shop, St Merryn. On the way Crusader sat in the back seat and I had just a little bit of that back seat. I said to Christopher: "I hope he don't bite me." He said: "I hope he don't bite me either!"

We drove on then, back to St Columb, where Marie was working as a nurse on night work. I got her to come out and see the dog. Poor old Marie, she just about had a heart attack. She thought we had a moorland pony on board. She said: "He's fully grown!" I didn't deny her statement. "Yes, yes, he is; fully grown." Which he wasn't. We left, and then we came home to Trevithick. When I walked him into the sitting room, my mother and father almost had heart attacks too. Mother said: "You'll have to take him back, he's a fully grown dog, it's too big for us." "No," I said: "It won't grow no bigger, Mother, this is it; everybody's had the pick of the bunch and we're left with just this one big one." "Well...all right," Mother says: "we'll see how it go." I knew in my mind, if he didn't bark and he behaved himself and I could keep him for three weeks, the rest of the family would fall in love with 'un. That's how I planned it.

It was always something I'd wanted, after watching a television series many years ago. It was a lifetime's ambition come true for me. I'd got my Pyrenean Mountain Dog. That night, I didn't bother to go to bed at all. I knew Crusader would need company, his first night in a new house. We were strangers. He knew Mrs Jory, how she talked, and what the routine was there. We had to learn his language and he had to learn ours. I remembered the things old Herbie Lyttleton* told me. It sounded a bit crude, but it really worked. Herbie said: "If you want a dog to be loyal to you, as soon as you get him let him smell your stockings, let him sleep with your stockings, or an old vest. When they smell the scent sweating from you," he said: "that's it for ever, they'll never leave you." And I did this. I know that night I had to take Crusader up into a field, just touching my house. It was about October time and the light wasn't all that good. I fell in a pothole; I thought I'd lost him and he'd run away. But he didn't, he stayed right by my side. He didn't know what to make of me. I got up and everything was all right.

When Marie came home the next morning, we had another big inquest about the dog. I told them he was fully grown. "He won't grow no more," I said: "In fact, he might start losing weight. They do," I said. I really convinced my family that Crusader would lose weight. Well, I tell you, we struggled to feed him, not financially (Marie was working), but to give him the things he wanted. But soon we overcame that.

But after a few days I realised that with Crusader I didn't have a healthy, strong dog. His bones used to crack and creak like a wicker basket. It was pitiful. He was lame in one leg. He really found it a struggle to even get out around with me. I took him to a veterinary and he had to take some medicine. I held his neck and my father tried to give it to him with a spoon. He just growled at us. It put the fear of God into my father and me as well. He said: "It's no good, he won't let us help him." I went back to the vet again and I had an X-ray done on his leg. The veterinary told me: "Mr Prynn," he said: "your dog has got something very bad with his leg." It was like a fracture in the bone. He said: "We can send him to the Research College at Bristol. It won't cost you anything and might repair it." I said to him: "Sir, I'll take him home and I'll live with it. Is he in pain?" "No," he said: "he isn't in pain. It's just the way he was born." I came home and I used to rub his legs, lay my hands on them.

*see Part I

I asked the Lord to let my dog be strong. If I couldn't see, 'please let my dog be really strong,' I said. I used to rub his legs until his eyes would glow. He'd be delighted with it. He'd twitch his nails and get a lot of pleasure out of this. But soon miracles happened for Crusader; that limp really went. I did see the veterinary again and he said he couldn't make it out, the way he'd got better. Well, I think the Lord helped me with that. He made my dog stronger, or I'll always believe so. It doesn't matter if nobody else does. He was well enough to take anywhere. The first place I decided on taking him was down to the beach. Dogs, they're like children, they love the beach. Crusader, I had him on the lead, he kept looking out to sea and walking along and digging great big holes. There was a giant excavator in Great Britain, in an open-cast coal site, called Big Geordie. Crusader was big, and he was digging holes in that beach just like Big Geordie was digging holes. He really loved it; it was just fun to Crusader. We walked along past Bloodhounds' Cove and headed over to a little bay, called June Bay. I decided, there was nobody else around, I'd let him run free, be on his own. He ran along just ahead of me. There's a point sticking out and then around the corner, was June Bay. The tide was very rough and going out and, as you know, waves will one minute cover the rocks and the next minute they'll go out and you can walk around. Crusader saw a little opening. He took off like a cart horse, like a bolting cart horse. I just couldn't catch him, it was impossible. He got a long way ahead of me and as he got near this point so some giant waves came in. I thought: 'Well, this is the end, tide going out and he's got out of his depth.' He could have been swept out to sea and there was nothing I could do about it, that sea's so strong. Crusader didn't know about it. He thought it was a place to have fun and games. He didn't realise it could be dangerous, but, by the Grace of God, he got around this corner. For the next five minutes, the waves just pounded in. I thought to myself: 'Well, if he gets right up, back of June Cove, he is safe.' But in the end the sea cleared from the point. I decided to take my chance and run around. There he was, right up in a corner, sitting down, waiting for me! Well, first, I can tell you I was absolutely furious when he did this, but when I had to wait to get to him I realised that it wasn't

Crusader's fault. You might wonder why I didn't give him a hiding or a beating. I could have. But I didn't 'cos it was all my fault. I was responsible for Crusader. He didn't know any better, but with my knowledge of the sea and dangers of it I should have known full well not to let him off the lead, but always to have him where I could be there to protect him. And after that, that was never to happen again. I was always careful.

We started to go wrecking in the evenings. Crusader got to know all the little places where I used to find wood. He used to pull on his lead and drag me right near a piece of wood or fish boxes or floats (they're round balls). I know, one night, I came away without my knife in my pocket, and I had a lot of rope and it was tangled up in an old pallet. I tried to cut it with a stone; it must have been about an inch-and-a-half thick, nigh on a hawser. And this is true, Crusader came for'ard and he sat down on his all-fours and shuffled up to the rope and, in about four or five champs, he nibbled right through the piece of rope for me. I put my arms around his neck and gave him a hug. I says: "Old man, I don't need a knife with you around, you've got things organised." It was always a favourite thing with Crusader, a champ-up, to cut a piece of rope in half. I often used to let him do it, sometimes just for fun. It didn't matter how tough anything was, Crusader was always there to help me out.

I know on one occasion we went wrecking one night about half-past-eleven ('cos Marie was on night shift). I'm like a blind-folded mule that knows where he's going: Crusader was leading me. But I did make a little bit of a boob, 'cos the sand had shifted and left a few rocks and I tripped and fell over. I thought I'd knocked my brains out. There he was, he came right forward to my face. I felt his big whiskers (they were as big as bristles on a hard broom), I felt them touch my face, as good as to say: "Well, come on, no good lying down here, up you come!' He was there to help me. But when you're wrecking, you can always pull more than you can carry; it doesn't matter if it's wood, rope or anything, and sometimes, if I had a rope and perhaps a couple of fish boxes, Crusader's favourite game was trying to get in them, or get on top and ride! Well, it was impossible. He used to stop as dead as a fish. I couldn't move, and the more I abused him the more he would wait his chance; if it was a piece of rope he'd get on the other end and it would be like a tug-o'-war. He'd be just like some of these big snow geese when they come in to land, they sort of ski along. Well, Crusader would get his big feet out and sort-of ski along the sand and I used to pull for a bit of fun. But I couldn't pull him very far, he was too heavy.

As the summer came, the weather got warmer and I used to take him out into the sea. I had a big, long lead. Well, his proper lead, and about twenty foot of rope. I used to let him go out and play in the water. If it was good weather, I used to take off my boots and I used to go out and paddle with him. He would try and race the waves, and then look at me and one great big one would come right in behind and just splash right over him, and then he'd gallop away! He'd gallop and turn and do little tricks, like a circus horse. As I knew all the special little rock pools, I used to take him along and go paddling. There was one in particular with a slate bottom, about six foot square and three foot deep. Well, Crusader measured about three foot six high, and the water used to come up almost to his chin. It was his favourite pool. He used to do all sorts of dancing. He would dance around in that pool just like dancing hailstones, and then stop, and have a rest and look at me. He would shake his head from one side to the other, just like a puppet on a string, while I was talking to him. A man can be silly who talks to his dogs, but I talked to Crusader, just like a human being. Crusader and I were as close together as David and Jonathan were. We hadn't signed any papers, but, mentally, we'd given ourselves to one another. My loyalty for Cru and his loyalty for me. We were buddies and it always stayed that way.

He was really big, maybe twelve, thirteen or fourteen stone. There were no bad legs on him; he stood firm on his legs as a North Sea Oil Rig. They're big and sturdy, those rigs are. So were Crusader's legs. He was big and massive. Water wheels are big, so was Crusader. He'd got a coat on him as white and thick as the snow on top of Mount Everest. He was just fantastic.

Crusader's favourite food was Cornish pasties. We have them twice a week. Mother always puts the initials of everybody's name on the pasties because each one has got different flavours, and so had Crusader's. He liked onion and plenty of pepper in his. One night, we had pasties for tea and my father said: "Well, that's the best pasty you've ever made for me." Mother replies: "It's the same one as you always have." But, when she came to give Crusader his pasty Mother says: "Jack, you've had the dog's pasty!" Everybody laughed. "Well," he said: "if that's the dog's pasty, he can have mine and I'll have his from now onward; I'm having the same flavour as what Crusader get." And that's just the way it was. My father and Crusader had the same flavours for their pasties.

When you're out with your dog you meet a lot of people. I've made many friends throughout Great Britain with my dog. People stopped their cars and had to talk to me about him. Sometimes wanted a photograph taken with him. Most probably some of you have seen Crusader but you didn't know he was my dog. One day I was down Shop, St Merryn, and a gentleman came up and talked to me about Crusader. He wanted to know all about him. He told me he was a photographer and he said: "Could I hire the dog for one day?" "Yes," I said: "you could." The gentleman did hire Crusader for a day. He paid me I think maybe eight pounds, and I signed a paper giving him the rights of the photographs. This man sends me calendars, postcards, each year with Crusader on them. He became a bit of a star, in a sense. He's gone all over the world, I know that: Western Europe, America and even Australia, on these calendars and cards. Sometimes in life funny little events happen!

I know all we humans have got little weaknesses; we're afraid of something or other. Well, Crusader was 'fraid of thunder and lighting. He really cried like a baby. It's the only time he was allowed to get on the bed; and I put down a little, small sheety thing for him. I put that right over the top of his head and he snuggled right in to me. He'd have three-quarters of the bed and I'd just have a quarter. He'd keep pushing, and push me out, trying to get closer. I held on to him and kept talking to him and telling him there was nothing to be worried about: "Crusader, I'm here. It's all right." And he'd really shake like a jelly-fish. He really did. Yes, old Crusader he was always really glad when the thunder and lightning passed over.

Some nights he dreamed and I heard 'in out on the landing, howling. Maybe he dreamed of some big siege in bygone days, of his ancestors, perhaps, fighting off wolves from a little crofters' village, or maybe he thought of Josie, his friend, a couple of doors away. Well, I'd shout and wake 'un up. Sometimes, during the night maybe I'd be dreaming, and he'd come in and wake me up; just put those great, big whiskers near my arms or my face — it was like switching on an electric light. Woke me right up.

When my son Christopher came home from abroad, I always told Crusader about three weeks before. I always said: "Christopher will be home in three weeks." Once more that old head would move from side to side like a puppet on a string. He was pleased, and he knew he was coming. So excited: he was really pleased when Christopher walked in the door. That old tail would flash and stand out straight; his tail was just like the branch of a pine tree. But like all holidays, when Chris is home time goes quickly (if a thing's good, it goes quickly); it was always sad for Crusader when he saw Christopher's case. He always went down to the bottom of the garden. He knew that he'd lost his wheels. I mean by that he'd lost his transport; no riding out in the car for another six months. He knew Chris had gone a long, long way away; he'd only listen to him by recordings; he didn't like that a little bit.

Some of you might say: 'Ed, you thought a lot of that dog. He meant everything to you. If someone had offered you a lot of money, would you have sold him?" The answer is: 'No, I wouldn't have sold him.' There's nobody in the world with enough money, to have bought that dog off me. I would have given him away if somebody was really ill and it would have made him well. It would have been a hard thing for me to do, a terrible pain to give Crusader away, but I could have done it. But I know none of you would have wished me to do that. You'd have wanted me and Crusader to be as close as David and Jonathan, as we'd always been.